PARADOXES

PARADOXES

R. M. SAINSBURY

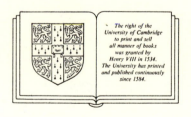

CAMBRIDGE UNIVERSITY PRESS
Cambridge
New York   New Rochelle   Melbourne   Sydney

Published by the Press Syndicate of the University of Cambridge
The Pitt Building, Trumpington Street, Cambridge CB2 1RP
32 East 57th Street, New York, NY 10022, USA
10 Stamford Road, Oakleigh, Melbourne 3166, Australia

First published 1988

Printed in Canada

Library of Congress Cataloging-in-Publication Data

Sainsbury, R. M. (Richard Mark)

Paradoxes.
Bibliography: p.
1. Paradox. I. Title.
BC199.P2S25   1987   165   87-23861

ISBN 0 521 33165 X hard covers
ISBN 0 521 33749 6 paperback

British Library Cataloguing-in-Publication Data applied for

CONTENTS

vi   Contents

ACKNOWLEDGMENTS

I would like to express my warm thanks to Jonathan Sinclair-Wilson of Cambridge University Press, who first suggested that I write this book, and who provided gentle and helpful encouragement and guidance throughout its preparation.

I am grateful to an anonymous referee for the Press, and to many friends, colleagues, and students for valuable comments and discussions.

I have borrowed liberally from other writers, and hope to have acknowledged them individually either in footnotes or the bibliographical notes found at the ends of chapters. If there is a case in which I have failed to do this, it is an inadvertence for which I apologize.

I am also grateful to members of the Philosophy Department and the Center for Cognitive Science at the University of Texas at Austin for stimulating discussion and for kindly providing technical resources for preparing the final manuscript. In addition, the Center generously allowed a font it had created to be used for typesetting some symbols that appear in the book.

INTRODUCTION

Paradoxes are fun. In most cases, they are easy to state and immediately provoke one into trying to "solve" them.

One of the hardest paradoxes to handle is also one of the easiest to state: the Liar Paradox. One version of it asks you to consider the man who simply says, "What I am now saying is false." Is what he says true or false? The problem is that if he speaks truly, he is truly saying that what he says is false, so he is speaking falsely; but if he is speaking falsely, then, since this is just what he says he is doing, he must be speaking truly. So if what he says is false, it is true; and if it is true, it is false. This paradox is said to have "tormented many ancient logicians and caused the premature death of at least one of them, Philetas of Cos."[1] Fun can go too far.

Paradoxes are serious. Unlike party puzzles and teasers, which are also fun, paradoxes raise serious problems. Historically, they are associated with crises in thought and with revolutionary advances. To grapple with them is not merely to engage in an intellectual game, but is to come to grips with key issues. In this book, I report some famous paradoxes and indicate how one might respond to them. These responses lead into some rather deep waters.

This is what I understand by a paradox: an apparently unacceptable conclusion derived by apparently acceptable reasoning from apparently acceptable premises. Appearances have to deceive, since the acceptable cannot lead by acceptable steps to the unacceptable. So, generally, we have a choice: Either the conclusion is not really unacceptable, or else the starting point, or the reasoning, has some nonobvious flaw.

Paradoxes come in degrees, depending on how well appearance camouflages reality. Let us pretend that we can represent how paradoxical something is on a ten-point scale. The weak or shallow

---

[1]   A. Tarski [1969], 66.

1

end we shall label 1; the cataclysmic end, home of paradoxes that send seismic shudders through a wide region of thought, we shall label 10. Serving as a marker for the point labeled 1 is the so-called Barber Paradox: In a certain remote Sicilian village, approached by a long ascent up a precipitous mountain road, the barber shaves all and only those villagers who do not shave themselves. Who shaves the barber? If he himself does, then he does not (since he shaves *only* those who do not shave themselves); if he does not, then he indeed does (since he shaves *all* those who do not shave themselves). The unacceptable supposition is that there is such a barber – one who shaves himself if and only if he does not. The story may have sounded acceptable: It turned our minds, agreeably enough, to the mountains of inland Sicily. However, once we see what the consequences are, we realize that the story cannot be true: There cannot be such a barber, or such a village. The story is unacceptable. This is not a very deep paradox because the unacceptability is very thinly disguised by the mountains and the remoteness.

At the other end of the scale, the point labeled 10, I shall place the Liar. This placing seems the least that is owed to the memory of Philetas.

The deeper the paradox, the more controversial is the question of how one should respond to it. All the paradoxes I discuss in the ensuing chapters score 6 or higher on the scale, so they are really serious. (Some of those in Appendix I should, I think, score lower.) This means that there is severe and unresolved disagreement about how one should deal with them. In many cases, though certainly not all (not, for example, in the case of the Liar), I have a definite view; but I must emphasize that, although I naturally think my own view is correct, other and greater men have held views that are diametrically opposed. To get a feel for how controversial some of the issues are, I suggest examining the bibliographical notes at the ends of chapters, where I identify my opponents.

Footnotes beginning with "**Q**" contain questions (though not necessarily in the first sentence). I hope that considering these will give pleasure and will prompt the reader to elaborate some of the themes in the text. Questions marked "**Q***" are referred to in Appendix II, where I have made either a point that might be relevant to an answer, or a suggestion for further reading.

I feel that Chapter 5 is the hardest and should be left until last. The order of the first four is somewhat arbitrary, and each has been written with the thought that it might be read first. Chapter 6 does not introduce a paradox, but rather defends the assumption, made in the earlier chapters, that all contradictions are unacceptable.

I face a dilemma: I find a book disappointing if the author does not express his own beliefs. What holds him back from stating, and arguing for, the truth as he sees it? I could not bring myself to exercise this restraint. On the other hand, I certainly would not want anyone to believe what I say without first carefully considering the alternatives. So I must offer somewhat paradoxical advice: Be very skeptical about the proposed "solutions"; they are, I believe, correct.

1. ZENO'S PARADOXES: SPACE, TIME, AND MOTION

1.1. INTRODUCTION

Zeno the Greek lived in Elea (a town in what is now southern Italy) in the fifth century B.C. The paradox for which he is best known today is probably the one told about Achilles and the tortoise. For some reason now lost in the folds of time, a race is arranged between them. Since Achilles can run much faster than the tortoise, the tortoise is given a head start. Zeno's astonishing contribution is a "proof" that Achilles can never catch up with the tortoise no matter how fast he runs and no matter how long the race goes on.

The supposed proof goes like this. The first thing Achilles has to do is to get to the place from which the tortoise started. However, the tortoise, although slow, is unflagging: While Achilles was occupied in making up his handicap, the tortoise has advanced a little bit further. So the next thing Achilles has to do is to get to the *new* place the tortoise occupies. While he is doing this, the tortoise will have gone on a little bit further still. However small the gap that remains, it will take Achilles some time to cross it, and in that time the tortoise will have created another gap. So however fast Achilles runs, all the tortoise need do in order not to be beaten is keep going – to make *some* progress in the time it takes Achilles to close the previous gap between them.

No one nowadays would dream of accepting the conclusion that Achilles cannot catch the tortoise. (I will not vouch for Zeno's reaction to his paradox: Sometimes he is reported as having taken his paradoxical conclusions quite seriously and literally as showing that motion was impossible.) Therefore, there must be something wrong with the argument. Saying exactly *what* is wrong is not easy, and there is no uncontroversial diagnosis. Some have seen the paradox as produced by the assumption that space or time is infinitely divisible, and thus as

5

genuinely proving that space or time is *not* infinitely divisible. Others have seen in the argument nothing more than a display of ignorance of elementary mathematics – an ignorance perhaps excusable in Zeno's time but inexcusable today.

The paradox of Achilles and the tortoise is Zeno's most famous, but there were several others. The Achilles Paradox takes for granted that Achilles can start running, and purports to prove that he cannot get as far as we all know he can. This paradox dovetails nicely with one known as the Racetrack, or Dichotomy, which purports to show that nothing can *begin* to move. In order to get anywhere, the argument goes – say, to a point one foot ahead of you – you must first get halfway there. However, to get to the halfway point, you must first get halfway to *that* point. In short, in order to get anywhere, even to begin to move, you must first perform an infinity of other movements. Since this seems impossible, it seems impossible that anything should move at all.

Almost none of Zeno's work survives as such. For the most part, our knowledge of what his arguments were is derived from reports by other philosophers, notably Aristotle. He presents Zeno's arguments very briefly, no doubt in the expectation that they would be familiar to his audience from the oral tradition that was perhaps his own only source. Aristotle's accounts are so compressed that only by guess-work can one reconstruct a detailed argument. The upshot is that there is no universal agreement about what should count as "Zeno's paradoxes," or about exactly what his arguments were. I shall select arguments that I believe to be interesting and important, and which are commonly attributed to Zeno, but I make no claim to be expounding what the real, historical Zeno actually said or thought.

Aristotle is an example of a great thinker who believed that Zeno was to be taken seriously and not dismissed as a mere propounder of childish riddles. By contrast, Charles Peirce wrote of the Achilles Paradox:

> this ridiculous little catch presents no difficulty at all to a mind adequately trained in mathematics and in logic, but is one of those which is very apt to excite minds of a certain class to an obstinate determination to believe a given proposition. ([1935], vol. 6, §177, p. 122)

On balance, history has sided with Aristotle, whose view on this point has been shared by thinkers as dissimilar as Hegel and Russell.

1. Zeno's Paradoxes: Space, Time, and Motion

I shall discuss three Zenonian paradoxes concerning motion: the Racetrack, the Achilles, and a paradox known as the Arrow. Before doing so, however, it will be useful to consider yet another of Zeno's paradoxes – one that concerns space. Sorting out this paradox provides the groundwork for tackling the paradoxes of motion.

1.2. SPACE

In ancient times, a frequently discussed perplexity was how something ("one and the same thing") could be both one and many. For example, a book is one thing (one book) but also many (words or pages); likewise, a tree is one thing (one tree) but also many (leaves, branches, molecules, or whatever). Nowadays, this is unlikely to strike anyone as very problematic. When we say that the book or the tree *is* many things, we do not mean that it is identical with many things (which would be absurd), but rather that it is made up of many parts. Furthermore, at least on the face of it, there is nothing especially problematic about this relationship of being made up of.[1]

Zeno, like his teacher Parmenides, wished to argue that in such cases there are not many things but only one thing. I shall not consider this argument as such, but I do wish to examine one of its ingredients. At one point, it seems as though Zeno is arguing along the following lines. Assume that space is infinitely divisible, in that there is no upper limit to the number of divisions of a space that could, in theory, be effected. Then every spatial volume or region has an infinite number of spatial parts. Each such part must then have some finite size, for these reasons:

(a) If it did not, it could not be said to exist, or to be spatial.
(b) Even infinitely many sizeless parts cannot form a space of some finite size: Adding nothings, however many, always results in nothing.

So (a) and (b) show that every spatial part must have some finite

---

[1] Q: Appearances may deceive. Let us call some particular tree *T*, and the collection of its parts at a particular moment *P*. Since trees can survive the loss of some of their parts (e.g., of their leaves in the fall), *T* can exist when *P* no longer does. Does this mean that *T* is something other than *P* or, more generally, that each thing is distinct from the sum of its parts? Can *P* exist when *T* does not (e.g., if the parts of the tree are dispersed by timber-felling operations)?

size. From this it seems to follow that not all spaces are infinitely divisible in the sense of containing an infinite number of spatial parts, because an infinite number of parts, each of some finite size, must form an infinitely large space.

This argument played the following role in Zeno's attempt to show that it is not the case that there are "many things." He was talking only of objects in space, and he assumed that an object has a part corresponding to every part of the space it fills. He claimed to show that, if you allow that objects have parts at all, you must say that each object is infinitely large, which is absurd. You must therefore deny that objects have parts. From this he went on to argue that *plurality* – the existence of many things – was impossible. I shall not consider this further argument, but will instead return to the one about space.[2]

Let us start by considering how one might convince oneself that any space has infinitely many spatial parts. Suppose we take a rectangle and bisect it vertically to give two further rectangles. Taking the right-hand one, bisect it vertically to give two more new rectangles. Cannot this process of bisection go on indefinitely? If so, any spatial area is made up of indefinitely many others.

Wait one moment! Suppose that I am drawing the bisections with a ruler and pencil. However thin the pencil, the time will fairly soon come when, instead of producing fresh rectangles, the new lines will fuse into a smudge. Alternatively, suppose that I am cutting the rectangles from paper with scissors. Again, the time will fairly soon come when my strip of paper will be too small to cut. More scientifically, such a process of physical division must presumably come to an end *sometime:* at the very latest, when the remainder of the object is no more than an atom (proton, hadron, quark, or whatever) wide.

The proponent of infinite divisibility must claim to have no such physical process in mind, but rather to be presenting a purely intellectual process: For every rectangle we can consider, we can also consider a smaller one having half the width. This is how we conceive any space, regardless of its shape. What we have to discuss now, therefore, is whether the earlier argument demonstrates that space cannot be as we tend to conceive it.

It might be thought to show this for the following reason: We all know that there are finite spaces, but the argument supposedly shows

2   Q*: Given as a premise that no object has parts, how could one attempt to argue that there is no more than one object?

that there are not. Therefore we must reject one of the premises that leads to this absurd conclusion, and the most suitable for rejection, because it is the most controversial, is that space is infinitely divisible. This premise supposedly forces us to say that either the parts of a supposedly infinitely divisible space are finite in size, or they are not. If the latter holds, then they are nothing, and no number of them put together will compose a finite space. If the former holds, putting infinitely many of them together will lead to an infinitely large space. Either way, on the supposition that space is infinitely divisible, there are no finite spaces. Since there obviously are finite spaces, the supposition must be rejected.

An initial point is that the notion of infinite divisibility remains ambiguous. On the one hand, to say that any space is infinitely divisible could mean that there is no upper limit to the number of imaginary operations of dividing we could effect. On the other hand, it could mean that the space contains an infinite number of parts. It is not obvious that the latter follows from the former. The latter claim might seem to rely on the idea that the process of imaginary dividings could somehow be "completed." For the moment let us assume that the thesis of infinite divisibility at stake is the thesis that space contains infinitely many nonoverlapping parts, and that each part has some finite size.

The most doubtful part of the argument against the thesis is the claim that a space composed of an infinity of parts, each finite in size, must be infinite. This claim is incorrect, and one way to show it is to appeal to mathematics. We could say: Let us represent the imagined successive bisections by the following series:

$$\frac{1}{2}, \frac{1}{4}, \frac{1}{8}, \ldots$$

where the first term ($\frac{1}{2}$) represents the fact that, after the first bisection, the right-hand rectangle is only half the area of the original rectangle; and similarly for the other terms. Every member of this series is a finite number, just as each of the spatial parts is of finite size. This does not mean that the sum of the series is infinite. On the contrary, mathematics texts have it that this series sums to 1. If we find nothing problematic in the idea that an infinite collection of finite numbers has a finite sum, then by analogy we should be happy with the idea that an infinite collection of finite spatial parts can compose a finite spatial region.[3]

This argument from mathematics establishes the analogous point about space (namely, that infinitely many parts of finite size may together form a finite whole) only upon the assumption that the analogy is good: that space, in the respect in question, has the properties that numbers have. However, this is controversial. For example, we have already said that some people take Zeno's paradoxes to show that space is not continuous, although the series of numbers is. Hence we would do well to approach the issue again: We do not have to rely on any mathematical argument to show that a finite whole can be composed of an infinite number of finite parts.

---

[3]   Q: Someone might object: Is it not just a *convention* in mathematics to treat this series as summing to 1? More generally, is it not just a convention to treat the sums of infinite series as the limit of the partial sums? Furthermore, if this is a mere mathematical convention, how can it tell us anything about space?

Readers with mathematical backgrounds might like to comment on the following argument, which purports to show that the fact that the series sums to 1 can be derived from ordinary arithmetic notions, without appeal to any special convention. (*Warning:* mathematicians tell me that what follows is highly suspect!)

The series can be represented as

$$x + x^2 + x^3 + \ldots$$

where $x = \frac{1}{2}$. Multiplying this expression by x has the effect of lopping off the first term:

$$x(x + x^2 + x^3 + \ldots) = x^2 + x^3 + x^4 + \ldots$$

Here we apply a generalization of the principle of distribution:

$$a\,(b + c) = (a\,b) + (a\,c).$$

Using this together with a similar generalization of the principle that

$$(1 - a)\,(b + c) = (b + c) - a\,(b + c)$$

we get:

$$(1 - x)\,(x + x^2 + x^3 + \ldots) = (x + x^2 + x^3 + \ldots) - (x^2 + x^3 + x^4 + \ldots)$$

Thus

$$(1 - x)\,(x + x^2 + x^3 + \ldots) = x$$

So, dividing both sides by $(1 - x)$:

$$x + x^2 + x^3 + \ldots \; = \; \frac{x}{(1 - x)}$$

So where $x = \frac{1}{2}$, the sum of the series is equal to 1.

There are two rather similar propositions, one true and one false, and we must be careful not to confuse them.

1.   If there is a finite size, and a whole contains infinitely many parts none smaller than this size, then the whole is infinitely large.
2.   If a whole contains infinitely many parts, each of some finite size, then the whole is infinitely large.

Statement (1) is true. To see this, let the minimum size of the parts be δ (say linear or square inches). Then the size of the whole is $\infty \times \delta$, which is clearly an infinite number. However, (1) does not bear on the case we are considering. To see this, let us revert to our imagined bisections. The idea was that however small the remaining area was, we could always imagine it being divided into two. This means that there can be no lower limit on how small the parts are. There can be no size δ such that all the parts are at least this big. For any such size, we can always imagine it being divided into two.

To see that (2) is false, we need to remember that it is essential to the idea of infinite divisibility that the parts get smaller, without limit, as the imagined process of division proceeds. This gives us an almost visual way of understanding how the endless series of rectangles can fit into the original rectangle: by getting progressively smaller.[4] The explanation for any tendency to believe that (2) is true lies in a tendency to confuse it with (1). We perhaps tend to think: *At the end of the series* the *last* pair of rectangles formed have some finite size, and all the other infinitely many rectangles are larger. Therefore, taken together they must make up an infinite area. However, there is *no such thing* as the last pair of rectangles to be formed: Our infinite series of divisions has no last member. Once we hold clearly in mind

---

4   In ridding oneself of any temptation to accept (2), it may be useful to reflect on the following obvious falsehood:

If every man loves some woman or other, then some woman or other is loved by every man.

Compare:

If every region is composed of infinitely many parts each of some finite size or other, then there is some finite size or other such that every region is composed of infinitely many parts of that size.

Readers trained in formal logic will recognize a quantifier-shift fallacy here. The conditionals have $\forall\exists$ antecedents and $\exists\forall$ consequents, but $\forall\exists$ does not entail $\exists\forall$.

that there can be no lower limit on the size of the parts induced by the infinite series of envisaged divisions, there is no inclination to suppose that having infinitely many parts entails being infinitely large.

The upshot is that there is no contradiction in the idea that space is infinitely divisible, in the sense of being composed of infinitely many nonoverlapping spatial parts, each of some finite (nonzero) size. This does not establish that space *is* infinitely divisible. Perhaps it is granular, in the way in which, according to quantum theory, energy is. Perhaps, to fill out the suggestion a little, there are small spatial regions that have no distinct subregions. The present point, however, is that the Zenonian argument we have discussed gives us no reason at all to believe this granular hypothesis.

This supposed paradox about space may well not strike us as very deep, especially if we have some familiarity with the currently orthodox mathematical treatment of infinity. Still, we must not forget that current orthodoxy was not developed without struggle, and was achieved several centuries after Zeno had pondered these questions. Zeno and his contemporaries might with good reason have had more trouble with it than we do. The position of a paradox on the ten-point scale mentioned in the Introduction can change over time: As we become more sophisticated detectors of mere appearance, a paradox can slide down toward the Barber end of the scale.

In any case, clearing this paradox out of the way is an essential preliminary to discussing Zeno's deeper paradoxes, which concern motion.

1.3.   THE RACETRACK

If a runner is to reach the end of the track, he must first complete an infinite number of different journeys: getting to the midpoint, then to the point midway between the midpoint and the end, then to the point midway between this one and the end, and so on. However, since it is logically impossible for someone to complete an infinite series of journeys, the runner cannot reach the end of the track. It is irrelevant how far away the end of the track is – it could be just a few inches away – so this argument, if sound, will show that all motion is impossible. Moving to any point will involve an infinite number of journeys, and an infinite number of journeys cannot be completed.

Let us call the starting point Z (for Zeno), and the endpoint $Z*$. The argument can be analyzed into two premises and a conclusion, as follows:

1. Going from Z to $Z*$ would require one to complete an infinite number of journeys: from Z to the point midway to $Z*$, call it Z_1; from Z_1 to the point midway between it and $Z*$, call it Z_2; and so on.

2. It is logically impossible for anyone (or anything) to complete an infinite number of journeys.

Conclusion : It is logically impossible for anyone to go from Z to $Z*$. Since these points are arbitrary, *all* motion is impossible.

Apparently acceptable premises, (1) and (2), lead by apparently acceptable reasoning to an apparently unacceptable conclusion.

No one nowadays would for a moment entertain the idea that the conclusion is, despite appearances, acceptable. (As before, I refrain from vouching for Zeno's own response.) Moreover, the reasoning appears impeccable. So for us the question is this: Which premise is incorrect, and why?

Let us begin by considering premise (1). First, we need to clarify. The idea is that we can generate an infinite series, let us call it the Z-series, whose terms are

$$Z, Z_1, Z_2, \ldots$$

These terms, it is proposed, can be used to analyze the journey from Z to $Z*$, being, supposedly, among the points that a runner from Z to $Z*$ must pass through en route. Note in particular that $Z*$ is not a term in the series; that is, it is not generated by the operation that generates new terms in the series – halving the distance that remains between the old term and $Z*$.

We can concede straightaway that the word "journey" has, in the context, some misleading implications. Perhaps "journey" connotes an event done with certain intentions, but it is obvious that the runner could form no intention with respect to most of the members of the Z-series, for he (or she) would have neither the time, nor the memory, nor the conceptual apparatus to think about most of them. Furthermore, he may well form no intention with respect to those he *can* think about. Still, if we explicitly set these connotations aside, then (1) seems hard to deny, once the infinite divisibility of space is granted;

for then all (1) means is the apparent platitude that motion from Z to $Z*$ involves traversing the distances Z to Z_1, Z_1 to Z_2, and so on.

Suspicion focuses on (2). Why should one not be able to complete an infinite number of journeys in a finite time? Is that not precisely what *does* happen when anything moves? Furthermore, is it not something that *could* happen even in other cases? For example, consider a view that Bertrand Russell once affirmed: He argued that we could imagine a person getting more and more skillful in performing a given task, so that he (or she) did it more and more quickly. On the first occasion, it might take him one minute to do the job, on the second, only a half a minute, and so on, so that if he performed the tasks consecutively he could complete the whole series of infinitely many in the space of two minutes. Russell said, indeed, that this was "medically impossible,"[5] but he held that it was *logically* possible: No contradiction was involved. If Russell is right about this, then (2) is the premise we should reject.

However, consider the following argument, in which the word "task" is used in quite a general way, so as to subsume what we have been calling "journeys."

> There are certain reading-lamps that have a button in the base. If the lamp is off and you press the button the lamp goes on, and if the lamp is on and you press the button the lamp goes off.
>
> Suppose now that the lamp is off, and I succeed in pressing the button an infinite number of times, perhaps making one jab in one minute, another jab in the next half-minute, and so on, according to Russell's recipe. After I have completed the whole infinite sequence of jabs, i.e., at the end of two minutes, is the lamp on or off? It seems impossible to answer this question. It cannot be on, because I did not ever turn it on without at once turning it off. It cannot be off, because I did in the first place turn it on, and thereafter I never turned it off without at once turning it on. But the lamp must be either on or off. This is a contradiction. (Thomson [1954]; cited in Gale [1968], p. 411)

Let us call the envisaged setup consisting of me, the switch, the lamp, and so on, "Thomson's lamp." The argument purports to show

---

5   [1936], p.143.

that Thomson's lamp cannot complete an infinite series of switchings in a finite time. It proceeds by *reductio ad absurdum:* We suppose that it *can* complete such a series, and show that this supposition leads to an absurdity – here the absurdity being that the lamp is neither on nor off at the supposed end of the series of tasks.

The argument is not valid, however. The supposition that the infinite series has been completed does not lead to the absurdity that the lamp is neither on nor off. Nothing follows from this supposition about the state of the lamp *after* the infinite series of switchings.

Consider the series of moments T_1, T_2, ..., each corresponding to a switching. According to the story, the gaps between the members of this T-series get smaller and smaller, and the rate of switching increases. At T_1 a switching on occurs, at T_2 a switching off occurs, and so on. Call the first moment after the (supposed) completion of the series T^*. It follows from the specification of the infinite series that, for any moment *in the T-series*, if the lamp is on at that time there is a later moment in the series at which the lamp is off; and vice versa. However, nothing follows from this about whether the lamp is on or off *at T^**, for T^* does *not belong* to the T-series. T^* is not generated by the operation that generates new members of the T-series from old: being a time half as remote from the old member as its predecessor was from it. The specification of the task speaks only to members of the T-series, and this has no consequences, let alone contradictory consequences, for how things are *at T^**, which lies outside the series.[6]

The preceding paragraph is not designed to prove that it is logically possible for an infinite series of tasks to be completed. It is designed to show only that Thomson's argument against this possibility fails. In fact, someone might suggest a reason of a different kind for thinking that there is a logical absurdity in the idea of Thomson's lamp.

Consider the lamp's button. We imagine it to move the same distance for each switching. If it has moved infinitely many times, then an infinite distance has been traversed at a finite speed in a finite time. There is a case for saying that this is logically impossible, for there is a case for saying that what we *mean* by average speed is simply distance divided by total time: So if speed and total time are finite, so must distance be. If this is allowed,[7] then Thomson was right to say

---

6   Q: Are we entitled to speak of "the first moment after the (supposed) completion of the task"?

that Thomson's lamp as he described it is a logical impossibility, even though the argument he gave for this conclusion was unsatisfactory.

This objection might be countered by varying the design of the machine. There are at least two possibilities. One is that the machine's switch be so constructed that if on its first operation it had to travel through a distance δ, on its next it needed only to travel through δ/2, then only through δ/4, and so on. Another is that the switch be so constructed that it travels faster and faster on each switching, without limit.[8,9] It is hard to find positive arguments for the conclusion that this machine is logically possible; but this machine is open neither to Thomson's objection, which was invalid, nor to the objection that it involved an infinite distance being traveled in a finite time. Therefore, until some other objection is forthcoming, we can (provisionally, and with due caution) accept this revised Thomson's lamp as a logical possibility. What's more, if *it* is a possibility, then there's nothing logically impossible about a runner completing an infinite series of journeys.[10]

Notice, however, that one does not need to establish outré possibilities, such as that of a Thomson's lamp that can complete an infinite number of tasks, in order to establish that the runner can reach

---

[7]   Perhaps it should *not* be allowed: Perhaps ordinary conventions that fix the meaning of "average speed" do not speak to the case when either time or distance is infinite. However, if we are to accept that a run can be divided into an infinite number of "tasks," this must be done in such a way that the total distance traveled is finite. So if the run is to be investigated in terms of machines like Thomson's lamp, we do well to consider alternative designs not involving infinite distances.

[8]   Q: Does this mean that it would have to travel infinitely fast in the end?

[9]   Q*: Does this mean that the switch would have to travel faster than the speed of light? If so, does this mean that the machine is *logically impossible*?

[10]   Q: Evaluate the following argument:
We can all agree that the series of numbers $\frac{1}{2}, \frac{1}{4}, \frac{1}{8}, \ldots$ sums to 1. What is controversial is whether this fact has any bearing on whether the runner can reach Z*. We know that it would be absurd to say that energy is infinitely divisible merely because for any number that is used to measure some quantity of energy there is a smaller one. Likewise, Zeno's paradox of the runner shows that motion through space should not be thought of as an endless progression through an infinite series. It is as clear that there is a smallest motion a runner can make as it is that there is a smallest spatial distance that we are capable of measuring.

Z*. The argument is supposed to work the other way: If even the infinite Thomson's lamp is possible, then there can be no problem about the runner.[11]

In the next section, I discuss a rather sophisticated variant of the Racetrack. The discussion may help resolve some of the worries that remain with this paradox.

1.4.   THE RACETRACK AGAIN

Premise (1) of the previous section had it that a necessary condition of moving from Z to Z* is moving through the infinite series of intermediate Z-points. In this rerun, I want to consider a different problem. It is that there appear to be persuasive arguments for the following inconsistent conclusions:

(a)   Passing through all the Z-points is sufficient for reaching Z*.

(b)   Passing through all the Z-points is *not* sufficient for reaching Z*.

We cannot accept both (a) and (b). The contradiction might be used to disprove the view that the runner's journey can be analyzed in terms of an infinite series, and this would throw doubt on our earlier premise (1).

Let us look more closely at an argument for (a):

> Suppose someone could have occupied every point in the Z-series without having occupied any point outside it, in particular without having occupied Z*. Where would he be? Not at any Z-point, for then there would be an unoccupied Z-point to the right. Not, for the same reason, between Z-points. And, *ex hypothesi,* not at any point external to the Z-series. But these possibilities are exhaustive. (cf. Thomson [1954]; cited in Gale [1968], p. 418)

---

[11]   In Thomson [1954] the supposed impossibility of Thomson's lamp is used to cast doubt on the view that we can correctly see the runner's race as the completion of an infinite series of tasks. This is considered in the next section.

In other words, if you pass through all the Z-points, you *must* get to Z^*. Contrasted with this is a simple argument against sufficiency – an argument for (b):

> Z^* lies outside the Z-series. It is further to the right than any member of the Z-series. So going through all the members of the Z-series cannot take you as far to the right as Z^*. So reaching Z^* is not logically entailed by passing through every Z-point.

The new twist to the Racetrack is that we have plausible arguments for both (a) and (b), but these are inconsistent.

The following objection to the argument for (a) has been proposed.[12] The question, "Where would the runner be after passing through all the Z-points?" can be answered "Nowhere!" Passing through all the Z-points is not sufficient for arriving at Z^* because one might cease to exist after reaching every Z-point but without reaching Z^*. To lend color to this suggestion, Paul Benacerraf invites us to imagine a genie who "shrinks from the thought" of reaching Z^* – to such an extent that he gets progressively smaller as his journey progresses. By Z_1 he is half his original size, by Z_2 a quarter of it, and so on. Thus by the time he has passed through every Z-point his size is zero, and "there is not enough left of him" to occupy Z^*.

Even if this is accepted,[13] it will not resolve our problem. The most that it could achieve is a qualification of (a): What would have to be said to be sufficient for reaching Z^* is not merely passing through every Z-point, but doing that and *also*(!) continuing to exist. However, the argument against sufficiency, if it is good at all, seems just as good against a correspondingly modified version of (b). Since Z^* lies outside the Z-series, even passing through every Z-point *and* continuing to exist cannot logically guarantee arriving at Z^*.

Part of the puzzle here lies, I think, in the exact nature of the correspondence that we are setting up between mathematical series and physical space. We have two quite different things: on the one hand, a

---

12   By Paul Benacerraf [1962], p. 774.
13   Q*: Can the following objection be met?
      Where is the runner when he goes out of existence? He cannot be at any Z-point since, by hypothesis, there is always a Z-point beyond it, which means that he would not have gone through all the Z-points; but if he goes out of existence at or beyond Z^*, then he reached Z^*, and so the sufficiency claim has not been refuted.

series of mathematical points, the Z-series, and on the other hand, a series of physical points composing the physical racetrack. A mathematical series, like the Z-series, may have no last member. In this case, it is not clear how we are to answer the question, "To what physical length does this series of mathematical points correspond?" That there is a genuine question here is obscured by the fact that we can properly apply the word "point" both to a mathematical abstraction and to a position in physical space. However, there *is* a genuine question, for lengths, as ordinarily thought of, have *two* ends. If a length can be correlated with a mathematical series with only *one* end, like the Z-series, this can only be by stipulation. So if we are to think of part of the racetrack as a length, a two-ended length, corresponding to the mathematically defined Z-series, a one-ended length, we can but stipulate that what corresponds to the physical length is the series from Z to Z*. Given this, it is obvious that traversing the length corresponding to the Z-series is enough to get the runner to Z*. On this view, the paradox is resolved by rejecting the argument for (b), and accepting that for (a) – modified, perhaps, by the quibble about the runner continuing to exist.

This suggestion can be strengthened by the following consideration. Suppose we divide a line into two discrete parts, X and Y, by drawing a perpendicular that cuts it at a point B:

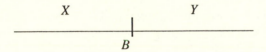

The notions of *line*, *division*, and so on are to be just our ordinary ones, whatever they are, and not some mathematical specification of them. Since B is a spatial point, it must be somewhere. So is it in X or in Y or both? We cannot say that it is in both X and Y, since by hypothesis these are discrete lines; that is, they have no point in common. However, it would seem that any reason we could have for saying that B is in X is as good a reason for saying that it is in Y. So, if it is in either, then it is in both, which is impossible.

If we try to represent the intuitive idea in the diagram in mathematically precise terms, we have to make a choice. Let us think of lengths in terms of sets of (mathematical) points. If X and Y are to be discrete (have no points in common), we must choose between assigning B to X (as its last member, in a left-to-right ordering) and assigning B to Y (as its first member). If we make the first choice, then Y has no first member; if we make the second choice, then X has no last member. So far as having an adequate model for physical space goes, there seems to be nothing to determine this choice – it seems that we are free to stipulate. However, what happens when we apply such a model to actual chunks of physical space?

Suppose we make the first choice, according to which B is in X. Imagine an archer being asked to shoot an arrow that traverses the whole of a physical space corresponding to X, without entering into any of the space corresponding to Y. There is no conceptual problem about this instruction: The arrow must be shot from the leftmost point of X and land at B. Now imagine an archer being asked to shoot an arrow that traverses the whole of a physical space corresponding to Y, without entering into any of the space corresponding to X. This time there appears to be a conceptual problem. The arrow cannot land at the point in space corresponding to B because, by stipulation, B has been allocated to X and so lies outside Y; but nor can the arrow land anywhere in Y, since for any point in Y there is one between it and B. There is no point that is the *first* point to the right of B.

What is odd about this contrast – the ease of occupying all of X and none of Y, the difficulty of occupying all of Y and none of X – is that *which* task is problematic depends upon a stipulation. If we had made the other choice, stipulating that B is to belong to Y, the difficulties would have been transposed.

Two real physical tasks, involving physical space, cannot vary in their difficulty according to some stipulation about how B is to be allocated. There is some discrepancy here between the abstract mathematical spacelike notions, and our notions of physical space.

If we think of X and Y as genuine lengths, as stretches of physical space, the difficulty we face can be traced to the source already mentioned: Lengths – for example, the lengths of racetracks – have *two* ends. However, if B belongs to X and not Y, then Y seems to lack a left-hand end: It cannot have B as its end, since B belongs to X and not Y (by hypothesis); but it cannot have any point to the right of B as its left end, for there will always be a Y-point to the left of any point that is to the right of B.

The difficulty comes from the assumption that the point B has partially to *compose* a line to which it belongs, so that to say it belongs to X and Y would be inconsistent with these being nonoverlapping lines. For an adequate description of physical space, we need a different notion: one that allows, for example, that two distinct physical lengths, arranged like X and Y, should touch without overlapping. We need the notion of a boundary that does not itself occupy space.

If we ask what region of space – thought of in the way we think of racetracks, as having two ends – corresponds to the points on the Z-series, the only possible answer would appear to be the region from Z to Z^*. This explains why the argument for sufficiency is correct, despite the point noted in the argument against it. Z^* does not belong to the Z-series, but it does belong to the region of space that corresponds to the Z-series.

In these remarks, I have assumed that we have coherent spatial notions – for example, that of (two-ended) length – and that if some mathematical structure does not fit with these notions, then so much the worse for the view that the structure gives a correct account of our spatial notions. In the circumstances, this pattern of argument is suspect, for it is open to the following Zeno-like response: The *only* way we could hope to arrive at coherent spatial notions is through these mathematical structures. If this way fails – if the mathematical structures do not yield all we want – then we are forced to admit that we were after the impossible, that there is no way of making sense of our spatial concepts.

The upshot is that a full response to Zeno's Racetrack Paradox would require a detailed elaboration and justification of our spatial concepts. This is the task Zeno set us – a task that each generation of philosophers of space and time rightly feels it must undertake anew.

1.5.   ACHILLES AND THE TORTOISE

We can restate this most famous of paradoxes using some Racetrack terminology. The Z-series can be redefined as follows: Z is Achilles' starting point; Z_1 is the tortoise's starting point; Z_2 is the point that the tortoise reaches while Achilles is getting to Z_1; and so on. Z^* becomes the point at which, we all believe, Achilles will catch the tortoise, and the "proof" is that Achilles, like the runner before him, will never reach Z^*.

We might see this as nothing more, in essentials, than the race-track, but with a receding finishing line. The paradoxical claim is this: Achilles can never get to Z^* because however many points in the Z-series he has occupied, there are still more Z-points ahead before he gets to Z^*. Furthermore, we cannot expect him to complete an infinity of "tasks" (moving through Z-points) in a finite time. An adequate response to the Racetrack will be easily converted into an adequate response to this version of the Achilles.

In such an interpretation of the paradox, the tortoise has barely a walk-on part to play. Let us see if we can do him more justice. One attempt is this:

> The tortoise is always ahead of Achilles if Achilles is at a point in the Z-series. But how is this consistent with the supposition that they reach Z* at the same time? If the tortoise is always ahead in the Z-series, must he not emerge from it before Achilles?

This makes for a rather superficial paradox. It is trivial that the tortoise is ahead of Achilles all the time until Achilles has drawn level: He is ahead until Z*. Given that both of them can travel through all the Z-points, which was disputed in the Racetrack but which is not now challenged, there is no reason why they should not complete this task at the same point in space and time. So I have to report that I can find nothing of substantial interest in this paradox that has not already been discussed in connection with the Racetrack.

1.6.   THE ARROW

At any instant of time, the flying arrow "occupies a space equal to itself." That is, the arrow at an instant cannot be moving, for motion takes a period of time, and a temporal instant is conceived as a point, not itself having duration. It follows that the arrow is at rest at every instant, and so does not move. What goes for arrows goes for everything: Nothing moves.

Aristotle gives a very brief report of this paradoxical argument, and concludes that it shows that "time is not composed of indivisible instants."[14] This is one possible response, though one that would currently lack appeal. Classical mechanics purports to make sense not only of velocity at an instant but also of various more sophisticated notions: rate of change of velocity at an instant (i.e., instantaneous acceleration or deceleration), rate of change of acceleration at an instant, and so on.

---

[14]   *Physics,* Z9. 239b 5.

Another response is to accept that the arrow is at rest at every instant, but deny that it follows that it does not move. What is required for the arrow to move, it may be said, is not that it move-at-an-instant, which is clearly an impossibility (given the semitechnical notion of *instant* in question), but rather that it be at different places at different instants. An instant is not long enough for motion to occur, for motion is a relation between an object, places, and various instants. If a response along these lines can be justified, there is no need to accept Aristotle's conclusion.

Suppose we set out Zeno's argument like this:

1.   At each instant, the arrow does not move.
2.   A stretch of time is composed of instants.
Conclusion: In any stretch of time, the arrow does not move.

Then the proposal is that this argument is not valid: The premises are true, but they do not entail the conclusion.

If the first premise is to be true, it must be understood in a rather special way, which provides the key to the paradox. It must be understood as claiming that the arrow does not move anywhere in the space of an instant. It must be understood in a way that admits of a further repudiation: a repudiation of the view that the way arrow and instant are related guarantees that the arrow is then at rest. The question of whether something is moving or at rest "at an instant" is one that essentially involves other instants. An object is at rest at an instant just on condition that it is at the same place at all nearby instants; it is in motion at an instant just on condition that it is in different places at nearby instants. Nothing about the arrow and a single instant alone can fix either that it is moving then or at rest then. In short, the first premise, if it is true, cannot be understood as saying that at each instant the arrow is at rest.

Once the first premise is properly understood, it is easy to see why the argument is fallacious. The conclusion that the arrow is always at rest says of each instant that the arrow is in the same place at neighboring instants. No such information is contained in the premises. If we think it is implicit in the premises, this is probably because we are failing to distinguish between the claim – interpretable as true – that at each instant the arrow does not move, and the false claim that it is *at rest* at each instant.

If this is correct, then the Arrow Paradox is an example of one in which the unacceptable conclusion (nothing moves) comes from an acceptable premise (no motion occurs "during" an instant) by unacceptable reasoning.

BIBLIOGRAPHICAL NOTES

Salmon [1970] contains the articles by Thomson and Benacerraf from which I drew the discussion of infinity machines, as well as many other important articles, including a clear introductory survey by Salmon. It also has an excellent bibliography. For a fine introduction to the philosophy of space and time, including a chapter on Zeno's paradoxes, see Salmon [1980].

For a historical account see Vlastos [1967]. For an advanced discussion, see Grünbaum [1967].

The quotation from Peirce, written late in his life, is not representative. In many other places, he discusses Zeno's paradoxes very seriously. However, it is not uncommon for people to see a paradox as trivial once they think they have a definitive solution to it. The cure for this reaction is to try to persuade someone else of one's "solution."

2. VAGUENESS: THE PARADOX OF THE HEAP

2.1. SORITES PARADOXES

Suppose two people differ in height by one-tenth of an inch (0.1 in.). Then, we are inclined to believe, either both or neither are tall. If one is 6 ft. 6 in. and the other is 0.1 in. shorter than this, then both are tall. If one is 4 ft. 6 in. and the other is 0.1 in. taller, then neither is tall. This apparently obvious and uncontroversial supposition appears to lead to the paradoxical conclusion that everyone is tall. Consider a series of heights starting with 6 ft. 6 in. and descending by steps of 0.1 in. A person of 6 ft. 6 in. is tall. By our supposition, so must be a person of 6 ft. 5.9 in. However, if a person of this height is tall, so must be a person one-tenth of an inch smaller; and so on, without limit, until we find ourselves saying, absurdly, that a person of 4 ft. 6 in. is tall; indeed, that everyone is tall.[1]

In ancient times, the standard version of this kind of paradox was told in terms of a heap, and the Greek word for "heap" – *sorites* – is now often used to demarcate all paradoxes of this general kind. Suppose you have a heap of sand: If you take away one grain of sand, what remains is still a heap. In general, removing a single grain can never turn a heap into something that is not a heap. Using the formulation of the previous paragraph: If two collections of grains of sand differ in number by just one grain, then both or neither are heaps. This apparently obvious and uncontroversial supposition appears to lead to the paradoxical conclusion that all collections of grains of sand, even one-membered collections, are heaps.

---

[1] This is a standard example in the literature, but it needs to be read with some caution. A person of 4 ft. 6 in. might be tall for a pygmy even though not tall for a Caucasian. We need to assume that the background class to which "tall" is relative is held constant throughout the example.

Suppose you are looking at a spectrum of colors through a device that divides the section of the spectrum you can see into two equal adjacent areas. Suppose the spectrum is so broad and the device so narrow that the colors in the two visible windows are always indistinguishable. Suppose further that the device is first placed at the red end of the spectrum, and then moved gradually rightward to the blue end. It is moved in such a way that the area that was visible in the right-hand window in the previous position is now visible in the left. At the beginning you will unhesitatingly judge that both areas are red. At each point, the newly visible area will appear indistinguishable from an area that you have already judged to be red and that is still visible. One is surely bound to the principle that if two colored patches are indistinguishable in color, then both or neither are red; yet clearly there must come a time when neither of the visible areas *is* red. This looks like a contradiction: On the one hand, no two adjacent areas differ in color and the first was certainly red; on the other hand, the first area differs in color from some subsequent color.[2]

What do these paradoxical arguments have in common? In each case, the key word is *vague:* "tall," "heap," "red." A vague word admits of borderline cases, cases of which the word is neither definitely true nor definitely false. There is no precise height that is enough for a person to be tall, and below which people are not tall; no precise number of grains that is enough for a collection to be a heap, and below which collections are not heaps; no precise position on the color spectrum separating all the red shades from the others. Consider contrasting *sharp* predicates. Let us define "tall*" to mean 6 ft. or taller: Then there is a sharp cutoff point. If you are 0.1 in. shorter than 6 ft., you are not tall*. Let us define "heap* of sand" to mean: a collection of at least 350 grains of sand: Then again there is a sharp cutoff. If you take away one grain from a 350-grained collection, you turn a heap* into a nonheap*. It is the vagueness of "tall" and "heap" that leads us to subscribe to versions of what one might call the "principle of tolerance": If two people differ in height by no more than 0.1 in., then both or neither are tall; if two collections of sand differ in number by at most one grain, then both or neither are heaps.

Vagueness must be distinguished from another phenomenon that I shall call *relativity*. Consider the property of *being above average in*

---

[2]   Q: How would one construct a parallel argument with the paradoxical conclusion that no men are bald?

height. Assuming that there is no problem about assigning numbers to people as measures of their height, this is not a vague property. A person is above average in height just on condition that the number that measures his or her height is greater than the number that measures the average height, and this is a completely precise condition. However, being greater than the average height, though precise, is *relative* to a given population. Being above average in height for a Swede involves being taller than does being above average in height for an Eskimo, since the average height of Swedes is greater than the average height of Eskimos.

As the example shows, relativity is different from vagueness, since it can hold of precise expressions, like "is above average height." Many vague predicates are also relative, but their relativity must not be confused with their vagueness. For example, "tall," unlike "above average height," is vague and also relative. You can see that the vagueness is different from the relativity by seeing that you could eliminate the relativity but leave the vagueness. If instead of "tall," we were to say "tall for a Swede," we would have eliminated the relativity, but the vagueness would remain. We believe that the difference of 0.1 in. cannot make the difference between being tall for a Swede and not. This means that the argument of the opening paragraph will work as well for "tall for a Swede" as it did for "tall."[3]

Vagueness must also be distinguished from *ambiguity*. Consider the word "bank." It can mean the edge of a river or a financial institution. As a result, there may be no one definite answer to the question "Did he go to the bank this morning?" So far, there is a parallel with vagueness. There may be no definite answer to the question "Is he bald?" if the person in question is a borderline case. However, there is a difference: In the case of ambiguity, a single sentence can be used to say, or ask, more than one thing. Before communication can proceed, the audience needs to determine *which* thing is being said or asked. In the bank example, there is no one answer because there is no one question. With vagueness it is different. If someone asks of a borderline case "Is he a child?", it is not that our problem in answering is the problem of knowing *which* question has been asked; there is only one possible question involved here. The problem is quite different: If the person of whom the question is asked is a borderline case, neither "Yes" nor "No" is a clearly correct answer. This question

---

[3]   Q: Is "heap" relative in the way that "tall" is?

has a single vague meaning, and that is quite different from having two or more meanings.

Vagueness is a widespread feature of our thought. Consider the following list: "child," "book," "toy," "happy," "clever," "few," "cloudy," "pearl," "moustache," "game," "husband," "table."[4] Is this feature ineradicable? Could we replace our vague expressions by precise ones? It is certain that precise expressions could not serve the same purposes as vague ones. Consider two examples of this.

The word "child" is vague. No moment marks the end of childhood. Leaving childhood is a gradual process. This fact is essential to the role that the concept *child* plays in our thought. For example, we take ourselves to have special duties to children that we do not have to adults, but these duties are not relinquished overnight; they gradually fade away. If we were to replace "child" by some more precise term, say "minor," as we have to for certain legal purposes, it would no longer be possible to express the obligations we feel. Our duties to a person as a child may end before or persist after his (or her) majority, depending on what age the law selects for coming of age, and depending on whether the person is, as we say, "old for his age" or "young for his age."

As another example, take the vague word "red." We could replace it by a precise expression, perhaps defined in terms of the physical reflectance properties of surfaces: Call this "red*." The trouble would be that we would have no use for "red*." "Red" is a word that we can reasonably apply on the basis of unaided observation. We can tell just by looking whether or not something is red; but this is not true of "red*." The best we could do would be to use some such rule as: If something is red, there is a good chance that it is red*. This would enable us to apply "red*" derivatively. However, application in this derivative way presupposes that we retain "red"; thus "red*" does not *eliminate* "red." Furthermore, "red*" does not serve the purpose of nonderivative applicability on the basis of observation that was served by "red."

It is one thing to say that vagueness cannot be eliminated from our thought and talk. It is another thing to ask whether vagueness is a genuine feature of reality, as opposed to something that emerges only from our ways of describing reality. According to one theory, reality

---

4   Q: Show that each of the words in the list is vague by briefly sketching a borderline case. Can you think of any words that are not vague?

itself is vague; according to another, it is just our descriptions that are vague, whereas reality itself is not. I return to this deep issue at the end of the chapter.[5]

As with any paradox there are three possibilities to consider:

(a) Accept the conclusion of the argument, but explain why it *seemed* unacceptable.
(b) Reject the reasoning as faulty.
(c) Reject one or more premises, explaining why they *seemed* acceptable.

In the case of vagueness, (a) seems a totally unpromising possibility to explore. Nothing could reconcile us to the suggestion that everyone is tall, or that a heap cannot be demolished grain by grain so that no heap is left, or that all colors are red. Moreover, the reasoning appears to be extremely simple and to use fundamental logical principles, so (b) is not very promising. However, let us pause to bring out in more detail one way in which the reasoning could go.

Suppose we start off with a collection of 10,000 grains of sand – something that is definitely a heap of sand. Let us write as our first premise:

1. A 10,000-grained collection is a heap.

Bearing in mind the tolerance principle, the next premise is this:

2. If a 10,000-grained collection is a heap, then so is a 9,999-grained collection.

Indeed, the tolerance principle generates numerous further premises of this form:

3. If a 9,999-grained collection is a heap, then so is a 9,998-grained collection.

And so on. Let us call the first premise the *categorical* premise and the

---

5 Q: How could one who holds that vagueness is not a feature of reality (but only of our descriptions of reality) respond to the following argument?

Mountains are part of reality, but they are vague. They have no sharp boundaries: It is vague where the mountain ends and the plain begins. So it is easy to see that vagueness is a feature of reality, and not just of our thought and talk.

others the *conditional* premises. (A conditional statement is one of the form "If ..., then ....")

We are just as inclined to hold to these conditional premises when they concern small numbers as when they concern large numbers, and just as inclined to hold to them for cases in which there is genuine doubt about whether a collection is heap-sized as when there is no such doubt. For example:

10,000.   If a 2-grained collection is a heap, so is a 1-grained collection.

We are firmly convinced that neither a 1-grained nor a 2-grained collection is a heap; but this does not stop us holding that *if* a 2-grained collection is a heap, then so is a 1-grained collection. We are reflecting our conviction that taking away a grain cannot turn something from a heap into a nonheap.

Similarly:

9,925.   If a 77-grained collection is a heap, so is a 76-grained collection.

Here we may be in genuine doubt about whether either collection deserves the name of "heap." However, the conditional reflects our confidence that both or neither are heaps, and this is simply another way of putting the tolerance principle: A difference of a grain cannot be the difference between a heap and a nonheap.

We do not yet have a paradox. To get it, we apply to these premises a general principle of reasoning: Given a proposition p, and a conditional of the form "if p, then q," we can derive q. This principle is still called by the Latin name it was given in the Middle Ages: *modus ponendo ponens*, or *modus ponens*, for short. Applying it to our first and second premises yields:

A 9,999-grained collection is a heap.

Applying the principle again to the above and premise (3) yields:

A 9,998-grained collection is a heap.

Continuing in the same way, we finally end up with the result that a 1-grained (or, for that matter, even a 0-grained) collection is a heap, and this is the absurdity.

The analysis reveals that the only principle of reasoning used in the derivation of the absurdity is *modus ponens*. It seems impossible to doubt this principle – impossible, that is, to suppose that it could ever lead us from truth to falsehood, no matter how often we apply it – so we are certainly reluctant to make response (b). Let us therefore investigate response (c): rejecting the premises, while explaining why they struck us as irresistible.

2.2.   REJECTING THE PREMISES: SUPERVALUATIONS

An initial reason for rejecting the premises is simply the unattractiveness of the other possible responses. If the conclusion cannot be swallowed, and if the principles of inference cannot be denied, then there *must* be something wrong with the premises. However, we would need to explain why the premises struck us as true.

Let us say that an object falls within the *positive extension* of a predicate, say "heap," just on condition that the object definitely possesses the relevant property, say, is definitely a heap; that it falls within the *negative extension* just on condition that it definitely lacks the property; and that otherwise it falls within the *penumbra*. By definition, a vague word is one for which some objects do, or could, fall within its penumbra. Using this terminology, let us consider one line of thought designed to explain why the premises of the paradoxical argument strike us as true, while not really being so.

A vague expression can be thought of as giving us some leeway with respect to the objects in its penumbra. These are objects that one is, as it were, at liberty to place in either the positive or negative extension, though one is not required to place them in either. We tend to exercise this license in the way shown by the tolerance principle; that is, we tend to think that if we have exercised it in one way with respect to an object, we must exercise it in the same way with respect to a closely similar one. However, when we are concerned with penumbral cases, this tendency is irrational. There is no question of a vague predicate being really true or really false of an object in its penumbra. We are at liberty to decide the matter either way. Therefore, in particular, there would be nothing wrong with placing a 5 ft. 10 in. man in the positive extension of "tall" and a man shorter than this by 0.1 in. in the negative extension. There is nothing that requires us to make any such choice; but equally there is nothing to rule it out. We are not in the realm of *how things are with the object;* rather, we are in the realm of *how we choose to speak of the objects*. Once we see this, so the line of thought goes, we see that the tolerance principle should not be adhered to, or at least should not be adhered to with respect to penumbral cases.

To reformulate the suggestion (I will keep to the "heap" example, but the suggestion is meant to apply generally): One speaks *truly* in applying "heap" to an object just on condition that the object is definitely a heap; one speaks *falsely* just on condition that the object is definitely not a heap. If one applies "heap" to an object in the penumbra of the word, one speaks neither truly nor falsely. The idea is to go on from this to show that the premises of the paradox are not all true.

Let us be clear about what more is required. The categorical premise does not apply to a penumbral object, and thus the present suggestion, quite rightly, leaves its truth untouched. So which premise is not true? No doubt it will be any premise dealing with objects that are penumbral for "heap": collections (we are pretending) with seventy or so members. However, these premises are *conditional* premises, and nothing that has so far been said entails anything about what it is for conditionals to be true, or false, or neither true nor false.

Suppose α and β are in the penumbra of "heap," and that α has one more grain than β. Then what has been said so far has it that "α is a heap" is neither true nor false; and likewise "β is a heap." However, what has so far been suggested does not speak to the question of whether or not the following conditional is true:

If α is a heap, then β is a heap.

For the suggestion to succeed in releasing us from the paradox, it has to show that some such premise is not true.

The needed refinement can be attained like this: "Heap" is vague, but it could be replaced by a sharp predicate. (Let us not now consider whether a sharp predicate could serve all the purposes the vague one serves.) Indeed, such replacement is the only way forward if someone relentlessly pursues the question, asked of a penumbral object, whether it is a heap or not. We have to say: There is no answer to *that* question, but we could introduce new predicates, rather like "heap," of which we *could* answer the question. Everything in the positive extension of "heap" will be in the positive extension of such a new predicate. Everything in the negative extension of "heap" will be in the negative extension of such a new predicate. Objects penumbral for "heap" will be distributed between the positive and negative extensions

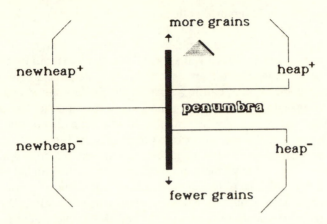

Figure 2.1. Sharpening the predicate "heap" by using the new predicate "newheap."

of the new predicates. There will be various ways of effecting the distribution, and one new predicate for each way.

In Figure 2.1, "heap$^+$" indicates the positive extension of "heap," "heap$^-$" its negative extension. "Newheap" is one of many new predicates that could be introduced, including in its positive extension the positive extension of "heap," in its negative extension the negative extension of "heap," and dividing between the extensions the collections penumbral for "heap." Such a predicate will be called a *sharpening* with respect to "heap."[6]

We can use the notion of a sharpening to give a fuller account of truth for sentences containing vague predicates. We will say that such a sentence is true if and only if it is true however its vague predicates are sharpened – in other words, if and only if the sentence is true for all sharpenings. What this means is best explained by examples.

---

[6] Q: The text is inaccurate (though the diagram will show in what way). For example, one way of distributing the penumbra of "heap" is as follows. The predicate "heap*" is defined to include the positive extension of "heap" in its positive extension, the negative extension of "heap" in its negative extension, and to include also in its positive extension the odd-numbered members of the penumbra of "heap" and in its negative extension the even-numbered members of the penumbra of "heap." Explain why this predicate would not serve the purposes in question. Give a fully accurate definition of a *sharpening*.

Suppose that a 75-grained collection, call it α, is in the penumbra of "heap." Some sharpenings of "heap" make "α is a heap" true. For example, one sharpening would take 75-grained and larger collections into its positive extension and all smaller collections into its negative extension. However, the sentence is not true for *all* sharpenings, for there is a sharpening, call it Σ, that takes all 76-grained and larger collections into its positive extension and all smaller collections into its negative extension. So the sentence "α is a heap" is not true for all sharpenings, and therefore, on the present account, is not true. This was the desired result. For analogous reasons, the sentence is also not false. So far we have made no progress, for we had already shown how the present line of thought would hold that applications of "heap" to objects in its penumbra would be neither true nor false. What the apparatus of sharpenings provides – and this is the whole point of introducing them – is a treatment of complex sentences, in particular conditional sentences. We need to find a way, on this line of thought, of denying truth to some of the premises of the paradoxical argument. The relevant premises are conditionals, so we need to explain why the conditionals are not true.

Suppose as before that α and β are in the penumbra of "heap." In particular, suppose that α is a 76-grained collection and that β is a 75-grained collection. Is the following sentence true for every sharpening?

S.   If α is a heap, so is β.

No – for consider the sharpening Σ. Since it takes all 76-grained and larger collections into its positive extension, "α is a heap" is true for Σ; but since Σ takes all 75-grained and smaller collections into its negative extension, "β is a heap" is false for Σ. A sentence of the form "if ..., then ..." cannot be true if the first clause – the antecedent – is true and the second – the consequent – is false. Thus S is not true for Σ and so is not true for all sharpenings; therefore, S is not true. Neither is it false, as analogous reasoning would show.[7]

It is not that, on this account, *any* sentence in which a vague predicate is applied to an object in its penumbra is neither true nor false. For example, the sentence

α is either a heap or not a heap

---

[7]   **Q**: How could it be shown that S is not false?

is true for all sharpenings, and so true. A sharpening draws the line somewhere: Wherever it draws it, α will either fall in the positive or the negative extension. Hence, for any sharpening, either "α is a heap" or "α is not a heap" is true for that sharpening. Therefore "α is a heap or α is not a heap" is true for every sharpening – that is, on the account, *true (simplicitur)*.

This completes the account. I call it the *supervaluational* account, since this is what it is called by one well-known proponent of the approach, Kit Fine.[8,9] In summary, it purports to dissolve the paradox by showing that not all the premises of the paradoxical argument are true. In particular, the principle of tolerance does not hold for penumbral cases. The license granted by a vague predicate permits us (though it does not require us) to take any penumbral object as a counterexample to the relevant principle of tolerance. One alleged merit of the account is that it preserves standard logic: For example, it brings all instances of "either *p* or not *p*" out true. So on this account we need have no truck with the response I labeled (b): giving up some logical principles.

I shall consider two objections to the supervaluational account. The first is that the account presupposes that there is a sharp line between the positive extension of a vague predicate and its penumbra. For example, so the objection goes, the account presupposes that there is a number *n* such that a collection of *n* grains is definitely a heap and a collection of *n* - 1 grains is not. The presupposition emerges in the definition of a sharpening.

It is certain that what is allegedly presupposed is false, at least for some predicates. One way to see this is to observe that there can be a contrast between *clear* borderline cases and others. For example, I think that a sixteen-year-old is a clear borderline case with respect to "child." However, there are also borderline cases of borderline cases: A fifteen-year-old is probably a borderline case of being a borderline case with respect to "child." There is no sharp boundary between

---

8   See Fine [1975]; see also Van Fraassen [1966]. These papers involve some technicalities. For an informal account of the underlying idea, see Dummett [1975], esp. pp. 256-7.

9   Q: Does the supervaluational account entail that the following is true:

"α is a heap" is true or "α is not a heap" is true?

What interesting point about the supervaluational treatment of "or" does the answer highlight?

positive extension and penumbra. To make the point another way, we could devise a new version of the paradox, like the old except that "is a heap" or "is a child" is replaced by "is definitely a heap" or "is definitely a child."[10] This shows that "is definitely a heap" and "is definitely a child" are vague, and hence that it is vague where the positive extensions of "heap" and "child" end and their penumbras begin.

The question, then, is whether the supervaluational account really presupposes that there are sharp boundaries where there are not. I think it does not, and is therefore immune to the objection. If there is no sharp boundary both between positive extension and penumbra and between penumbra and negative extension, then the notion of a sharpening is vague. For example, suppose that a 100-grained collection is neither definitely in the positive extension of "heap" nor definitely in its penumbra. Then a predicate that takes 100-grained collections into its negative extension will be a borderline case of a sharpening. It will not definitely be a sharpening, since it is not definitely legitimate to treat 100-grained collections as if they were in the penumbra of "heap." It will not definitely *not* be a sharpening, since it is not definitely illegitimate so to treat 100-grained collections. Since, on the supervaluational account, truth is defined in terms of sharpenings, truth will itself be vague, on this account. This is one way in which the account could deal with the phenomenon under discussion – higher-order vagueness, as it is called.[11]

To show that higher-order vagueness does not destroy the supervaluational account's power to block the paradoxes, consider the following fact. For some number n, both n-grained and $(n-1)$-grained collections are definitely penumbral for "heap." So it is definitely the case that some sharpening – however little license we allow ourselves about what is to count as a sharpening – takes the larger collection into its positive extension, the smaller collection into its negative extension, and thereby falsifies the conditional:

> If the n-grained collection is a heap, so is the $(n-1)$-grained collection.

---

[10] Q: Write out the categorical premise of a paradoxical argument of this kind, and give one example of the conditional premises. What is the unacceptable apparent consequence of these premises?

[11] Q: Many sharpenings are quite definitely sharpenings. What example could you give to illustrate this?

Hence the vagueness of "sharpening" does not affect the fact that, on the supervaluational account, not all the premises of the paradoxical argument are true.[12]

I now turn to the second objection to the supervaluational account: that the account distorts the nature of vagueness. This objection requires some background.

Consider the word "pearl." This is vague (or so I shall pretend) for the following reason. Anything made of the correct material and formed in an oyster counts as a pearl. Anything not of the right material is not a pearl. However, there are borderline cases. What should we say of a pearl-shaped lump of pearl-material that has somehow been synthesized outside of any oyster? I suggest that the sense of "pearl" does not settle this question; so "pearl" counts as vague, but its vagueness is very different in kind from that of "heap" or "tall" or "child."

One difference is that an arbitrary decision to sharpen "pearl" in one way or another, to include or exclude these pearl-shaped lumps of pearl-material, would leave us with a sharp word capable of playing much the same role as our actual vague word "pearl." However, this is, at best, the sign of another, more important difference.

Suppose a parent says: "On no account may you wear your hair in a plait." This order speaks only to the style of the child's hair, not to its color. The parent does not say that he or she is indifferent to color; he or she simply does not mention it at all. So far as this order goes, the child has license with respect to color, though the order does not grant this license. By contrast, the order "On no account may you wear your hair in a plait, though you may color it any color you like" expressly grants license with respect to color. The meaning of a word is a bit like an order or a rule. I claim that the meaning of the word "pearl" is like the first kind of order. Just as the first kind of order did not speak to hair color, so the meaning of "pearl" does not speak to pearl-sized lumps of pearl-material. We end up with license with respect to these

---

12   Q: How would you assess the following objection to the present version of the supervaluational account?

If "sharpening" is vague, then no sentence can be definitely true. Truth involves appeal to *all* sharpenings; what is to count as a sharpening is vague, so it is not definitely true of any collection that these are all the sharpenings there are (with respect to a given predicate). However, it is absurd to suggest that "Yul Brynner was bald" is anything other than *definitely* true.

things, though that license is not expressly granted by the meaning of the word. By contrast, I shall claim that the meaning of words like "heap" does say something about penumbral cases, though what it says is not merely that one has license.

I shall elaborate and defend this claim. First, some terminology: I shall call words like "pearl," whose meaning is silent about penumbral cases, *inessentially vague*. I shall call words like "child," whose meaning speaks to penumbral cases, *essentially vague*.[13]

What does the meaning of an essentially vague word say about its penumbral cases? Let us first see what answer one can give on behalf of the supervaluational theory. There are two possibilities:

1. One can say that the answer is "Nothing," so that the license needed to justify the notion of a sharpening is granted by default, as in the first kind of order. This makes the supervaluational theorist deny the distinction between essential and inessential vagueness, or else affirm that every case of vagueness is a case of inessential vagueness.

2. One can say that the meaning expressly grants you a license to apply or deny the predicate, as you wish, on the pattern of the second kind of order.

Both of these possible answers are, in my view, wrong.

First of all, I think it can be shown that we have to allow that the meaning of an essentially vague predicate says something about its penumbral cases. If this is granted, the first possible answer is blocked. One argument for granting it is this: It follows from the meaning of "heap" alone that if α is a borderline case of a heap and β is a collection with more grains than α, then β is a better case of a heap than α. So the meaning of "heap" says *something* about borderline cases of heaps, unlike the meaning of "pearl" and borderline cases of pearls.

Second, it also follows from the meaning of "heap" that one would not be quite right, and nor would one be quite wrong, to call a borderline case a heap. This conflicts with the second possible response open to the supervaluational theory. If I am looking for some material

---

[13] Q: In all the examples I have given of of essential vagueness, there is a smooth progression: There are changes too small to make a difference to whether the word applies, though a large change does make a difference. Could one use this feature to *characterize* essential vagueness?

to match my red curtains, you would not be quite right if you said of material that is a borderline case of red, "This is red too," or "This will match." If the red crabs and only the red ones are good to eat, the rest being poisonous, and we are looking for our supper, you would not be quite right to say of a borderline case of red, "This is red" or "This is good to eat." The license that the supervaluational theorist seems to think is granted by even essentially vague predicates, with respect to how we apply them to borderline cases, appears to be illusory.

If we reflect on the following sentence, we shall see that the supervaluational account must be wrong.

> For some number n, an n-grained collection is a heap but an $(n-1)$-grained collection is not.

We believe that this sentence is false (and likewise similar sentences for other essentially vague predicates). Indeed, that it is false is a paramount sign that the predicate in question is vague: Vagueness is a matter of there being no sharp boundary. However, on the supervaluational theory the sentence comes out as true, since all its sharpenings are true.[14] This is unacceptable.[15]

Admittedly, the very strategy of the supervaluational theory was to make us give up something we inclined to believe, for we inclined to believe all the premises of the paradoxical argument. However, it is one thing to give up some of the conditional premises relating to

---

[14] Q: Why.is this the case? (Cf. Sanford [1976].)

[15] Various writers have suggested that it *is* acceptable, as long as we realize that the truth of the displayed sentence does not require that there be a number n such that the following is true:

an n-grained collection is a heap but an $(n-1)$-grained collection is not.

See, e.g., Dummett [1975], pp. 257-8; and, for opposition, Kamp [1981], p. 237ff. The claim depends upon two features: (1) a view of "there is" according to which it is like "or" [so that to say that there is a student who smokes is to say that either Sally smokes, or Michael smokes, or ... (and so on through all the students)]; and (2) a view of "or" according to which a statement "p or q" can be (definitely) true even though neither "p" nor "q" is. A standard alleged example of the latter is "This is orange or red," said of a borderline case. See again Dummett [1975], p. 255. It is not at all clear whether the combination of (1) and (2) is less paradoxical than the paradox of the heap. Put baldly, it involves saying that "there is a such-and-such" can be true, even if the result of saying, concerning each thing in the universe, that *it* is such-and-such, is in every case false.

penumbral cases ("if α is a heap, then β is a heap," etc.) – perhaps this, if well-motivated, would be tolerable. It is quite another thing to give up the very essence of vagueness – namely, that there are no sharp boundaries.

The supervaluational theory sees vagueness as a deficiency in the meaning of the vague word, a deficiency that needs to be put right. Moreover, the theory holds that, for example, the following is true:

>   Either this is a pearl or it is not.

Perhaps we can accept this. "Pearl" in not an essentially vague predicate. Perhaps accepting the displayed sentence is like agreeing that we need to make a *decision* about whether to count pearl-shaped lumps of pearl-material as pearls or not. Perhaps we can see this as rectifying a deficiency in the meaning of "pearl." However, contrast:

>   Either he is an adult or he is not.

Think how this might function in the following argument:

>   Either he is an adult or he is not. If he is an adult, then watching the hard-porn movie will do him no harm. If he is not an adult, then he will not understand it, so, in this case too, watching it will do him no harm. Either way, it will do him no harm to watch it.

We might object: The argument fails to take account of the person on the borderline between childhood and adulthood. For him, it is not right to say "Either he is an adult or he is not." There is certainly no question of settling this by a *decision,* and it is precisely because he is between childhood and adulthood that seeing the movie might harm him.

2.3.   REJECTING THE REASONING: DEGREES OF TRUTH

Let us take stock. We envisaged three possible responses to the paradox:

(a)   to accept the conclusion;
(b)   to reject the reasoning; or
(c)   to reject one or more premises.

We have taken (a) to be a nonstarter. We have explored how one might respond in fashion (c): This is the category to which the super-valuational theory belongs. I have not shown that there is no other (c)-type response, but I have argued that the supervaluational one is unacceptable. I now want to turn to a (b)-type response. As I said earlier, we are strongly disinclined to allow that there could be anything wrong with *modus ponens*. Nevertheless, some theorists have tried to place the blame on this principle of reasoning, and I will try to explain their grounds.

When asked to assess a claim to the effect that a sixteen-year-old is an adult, it is natural to say something like "That's *to some extent* true," or "There's *a certain amount of truth* in that"; likewise whenever a vague predicate is applied to an object in its penumbra. The response to the paradoxical argument I now wish to consider takes this very seriously. The suggestion is that we introduce the idea of *degrees of truth*. Applying a predicate to an object in its positive extension will rate the highest degree of truth, conventionally 1. Applying a predicate to an object in its negative extension will rate the lowest degree of truth, conventionally 0. Applying a predicate to an object in its penumbra will rate a degree of truth lying somewhere between these two extremes. Where the value lies will show where the object lies in the penumbra, relative to the positive and negative extension. Thus ascribing "bald" to a man who nearly qualifies as bald will rate a degree of truth closer to 1 than applying it to a man who nearly qualifies as nonbald. A degree of truth theory thus takes very seriously the point that the meaning of an essentially vague word says something about the borderline cases. The theory seeks to represent *what* the meaning says by the various degrees of truth.

How can a degree theory dissolve the paradoxical argument? It must assign the highest degree of truth to the categorical premise of the argument and the lowest degree to the conclusion; but how will it treat the conditional premises?

Suppose collections of grains of sand start becoming penumbral for "heap" at around the 100 mark. Consider the following conditional:

> If this 95-grained collection is a heap, so is this 94-grained collection.

What should the degree theorist say? The antecedent of the conditional is

> This 95-grained collection is a heap.

The consequent is

> This 94-grained collection is a heap.

According to the degree theory, the antecedent is nearly but not quite true. Perhaps it is assigned the degree of truth 0.96. The consequent is also nearly true, but not quite so nearly true as the antecedent. Perhaps it is assigned the degree of truth 0.95. What degree of truth should be assigned to the conditional itself?

There is room for variation in detail, but the general idea is that if the antecedent of a conditional is truer than its consequent, then the conditional cannot be wholly true; thus the conditional in question needs to be assigned a degree of truth less than 1. The justification for this lies in part with the analogy with the standard case in which degrees of truth are not taken into account: We say that a conditional whose antecedent is true and whose consequent is false cannot be true, because a conditional should not lead from truth to falsehood. Analogously, a conditional should not lead to a lower degree of truth. The greater the amount of truth lost in the passage from antecedent to consequent, the lower the degree of truth assignable to the whole conditional.

It might seem, then, as if the degree theorist's response is of type (c): reject the premises. On this theory the conditional premises, though very nearly true, are not quite true. Hence we need not be fully committed to them. Hence the paradoxical argument does not commit us to the paradoxical conclusion. However, this would not be a good account. Even if we are not fully committed to the premises, they are very nearly true. The degree theorist has to explain how premises that are all very nearly true can lead to a conclusion that is wholly false.

To do this, the theorist must challenge the validity of *modus ponens,* and this is what makes the response of type (b): reject the reasoning. On the degree-theoretic account, *modus ponens* does not preserve degree of truth: The conclusion of an argument of the form "If p, then q; p, therefore q" may have a lower degree of truth than any of the premises. Revert to the conditional about 95- and 94-grained heaps. This conditional itself is extremely close to the whole truth: Perhaps it has a truth degree of 0.99. The antecedent, we suggested, had truth degree 0.96. Yet applying *modus ponens* yields a conclusion with truth degree only 0.95, lower than the truth degree of either of the premises. *Modus ponens* is valid as applied to sentences with the extreme truth degrees, 0 or 1: One cannot get a conclusion with degree less than 1 from premises of degree 1. However, in the intermediate degrees the application of *modus ponens* can lead to a "leakage" of truth. The leakage may be small for each application, but can be large if the number of applications is large, as in the case of the paradoxical argument.

We earlier thought that *modus ponens* was a principle that simply could not be abandoned. The abandonment suggested by the degree theorist, however, may well be consistent with all we really believed about *modus ponens*. We had in mind only the cases in which it was applied to sentences that were (*completely*) true or (*completely*) false. For these cases, the degree theorist's view agrees with our intuitions. It is simply not clear whether or not our intuitions spoke to cases of *partial* truth, so it is not clear that there is anything counterintuitive about the degree theorist's proposal.

A full defense of the degree of truth theory would require the consideration of a number of issues that I shall briefly mention. First, it is necessary to say something about what a degree of truth is. Second, some account must be given of the source and justification of the numbers that are to be assigned as degrees. Third, the full implications of the degree theory for logic must be set out and defended.

A key property of truth is marked by the platitude that we aim to believe what is true. If we could show that degrees of truth had an analogous property, we would have gone some way toward explaining what a degree of truth is.

Suppose that you are fairly sure that Arkle won the Gold Cup in 1960. Your memory may fail you about some matters, but you are pretty reliable about the history of the turf. You reckon that you have a very much better than fifty–fifty chance of being right that it was Arkle. Then, if you are at all attracted by gambling, it will be rational for you to bet on his having won if you can get odds as good as even: If you follow this policy generally, you will win more than fifty times out of a hundred. Say that each time you win, you gain a dollar, and each time you lose, you lose a dollar. A policy that will result in your winning more than you lose is a policy that it is rational for you to pursue. It is rational to perform a particular action that is required by the pursuit of a rational policy.

We want to believe what is true, but we do not always know what is true. The greater the confidence we have in a proposition, the more it affects us as if we believed it to be true. If we are almost certain that our house will not burn down, we will not spend much money insuring it against fire. If we are almost certain that we shall be alive tomorrow, we do not waste much time today making arrangements for our death.

It is rational, then, for our beliefs to vary in strength, reflecting variations in our confidence, and thus variations in our assessment of the quality of our information. We may be less than totally confident because we are less than fully informed. Here, the less than total confidence mirrors our deficiencies.

Vagueness may also lead to less than total confidence. Suppose you know, having had it on impeccable authority, that all and only red mushrooms are poisonous. You wish to kill Jones. All other things being equal, you would prefer to poison him, and you would prefer to do so using mushrooms, so that it will look like an accident. However, the only mushroom you can find right now, though reddish, is not a clear case of red. Will you use it to try to poison Jones? It depends upon how important it is to you to succeed, how important it is to succeed at first attempt, and how soon Jones must die if his death is to be of service to you. The lower the weight you assign to these factors, the more reasonable it becomes to use the mushroom. The higher the weight, the less reasonable. The more confident you are that this mushroom is really red, the more reasonable it is to use it; the less confident, the less reasonable. In the context, this confidence affects your action in the same way as would a lack of confidence springing from lack of information, from fear that your memory fails you, or whatever. From the point of view of action, it is rather as if you had less than total confidence in the statement "This mushroom will do the job."

However, there is also a sharp contrast. Less than total confidence springing from incomplete evidence or fear of unreliability mirrors our deficiencies; less than complete confidence springing from an appreciation of vagueness does not. If the mushroom is a borderline case, it is not your fault that you are unsure whether it should be counted as red; indeed, you would be at fault if you firmly classified it either as red or as not red. No matter how perfect your memory and senses, no matter how infallible your reasoning, the mushroom stays on the borderline. On the question of whether the mushroom is red, an omniscient being could do no better.

Where we have incomplete information, or unreliability, there is a chance of improvement: We can in theory raise our confidence by getting more information. Where we have vagueness, there may be no chance of improvement: Given your language and the way the world is, you can do no better than have partial confidence in "This mushroom is red." Truth is what we seek in belief: It is that than which we cannot do better. So where partial confidence is the best that is even theoretically available, we need a corresponding concept of partial truth or degree of truth. Where vagueness is at issue, we must aim at a degree of belief that matches the degree of truth, just as, where there is no vagueness, we must aim to believe just what is true.

The second part of a defense of a degree of truth theory is to explain and justify the origin of the numbers that are assigned as degrees of truth. Suppose there are two mushrooms, both borderline cases of red, but one redder than the other. If you want to commit the poisoning, and you have full confidence in the information that all and only red ones kill, you will choose the redder if you choose either: The redder one must be closer to being a definite case of red. This suggests how we could justify assigning degrees of truth: We have to assign a higher degree to a redder object; or, if we are dealing with "heap," we must assign a higher degree to penumbral collections the more numerous they are. In short, the source and justification of assignments of degrees of truth would lie in our comparative judgments involving penumbral cases.[16,17]

The third part of the defense of a degree theory would involve justifying the logic that issues from it. Such a theory leads to a departure from ordinary, so-called classical, logic. Whereas classical logic has it that all sentences of the form "σ and not-σ" are false, and all sentences of the form "σ or not-σ" are true, the degree theorist demurs. When σ has only a medium degree of truth, "σ and not-σ" will not be completely false, and "σ or not-σ" will not be completely

---

[16] Q: How would you respond to the following objection?

It is one thing to say that the comparative form of "red," viz. "redder than," is to be used as the basis for assigning degrees in connection with "red"; but it is quite another thing to apply this to "heap." The basis for the assignments would be comparisons involving "heaper than"; but this is nonsense.

[17] Q: How would you respond to the following objection?

I agree that there are degrees of redness, but I cannot see that this means that there are degrees of truth.

true.[18] We have already seen, in the case of the argument about the harmful effects of watching hard-porn movies, that there is at least some case for holding that, if σ is vague, "σ or not-σ" is not without qualification true. Furthermore, the naturalness of "It is and it isn't," as a response to the question whether a borderline-case mushroom is red, gives at least a preliminary indication that the degree theorist is right to recognize that not all instances of "σ and not-σ" are completely false.

The degree theory dissolves the paradox, and is in my view defensible. However, even if the paradox is dissolved, it would be a pity to leave the topic of vagueness without raising this fundamental, albeit obscure, question: Are there vague *objects*, or is vagueness something that arises, not from the way the world itself is, but rather from how we describe it?

2.4.   VAGUE OBJECTS?

We can start by reverting to an earlier question (see footnote 5). The argument for discussion went like this:

> Mountains are part of reality, but they are vague. They have no sharp boundaries: It is vague where the mountain ends and the plain begins. So it is easy to see that vagueness is a feature of reality, and not just of our thought and talk.

Even if we like the conclusion, we should not accept this argument for it. Given our language, which contains words like "mountain," we can ask a vague question: Does this spot belong to the mountain or to the plain? However, it is far from obvious that we need such a word in order to give a complete account of what there is in the world. If we do not need the word, then perhaps the vagueness it introduces does not lie in the world. Here it is worth remembering that a word like "heap" certainly does not require us to recognize the existence of vague objects. Each collection of grains has a completely definite number of grains: We do not have to use the vague word "heap" to describe what there is. So, for all that has been said, there is room for the view that vagueness comes from our thought and talk, and is not an objective feature of the world.

---

[18] Fine [1975] shows informally how the degree theorist is committed to such departures from classical logic.

Let us consider an old story. Theseus had a ship. When a plank rotted, it was replaced. After a while, none of the original planks was left. Likewise for the other kinds of parts of the ship – masts, sails, and so forth. Did Theseus' ship survive? Suppose that someone had kept the rotted planks and other parts and then reassembled these into a (doubtless unseaworthy) ship. Does this have a better claim to be the original ship of Theseus? There is vagueness of some kind here. The question is: Is the ship *itself* vague, or does the vagueness end with the word "ship," leaving the ship itself uncontaminated?

It seems to me that the second answer is the right one. In such a case, we can give an agreed and relatively precise account of the "facts of the matter." We know just what happened. It is a verbal question to which object, if any, we ought to apply the phrase "the ship of Theseus."

This view could be supported by an argument with the following structure. First, show that *identity* is not a vague relation; that is, show that questions of the form "Is this thing (perhaps, Theseus' original ship) the same as that thing (perhaps, the ship later reassembled from the parts of Theseus' original)?" have definite answers. The suggestion is that, quite generally:

If β is α, then β is definitely α.

This is supposedly shown by the reflection that it seems indisputable that, for any object α,

α is definitely α.

Suppose β is α. Anything true of α is true of β. "Is definitely α" is true of α; so "is definitely α" is true of β. Hence:

β is definitely α.

The second step of the argument involves showing that if identity is not a vague relation, then objects are not vague. The idea is that if an object were vague, it would be a vague matter what object it is identical with. Since the first part of the argument has supposedly shown that identity is not vague, the conclusion is drawn that objects are not vague.

I close with two qualms. First, denying that there are vague objects seems to presuppose that the "facts themselves" are precise. I said that, in the case of Theseus' ship, the facts of the matter are "relatively precise." They are precise relative to the vagueness of "ship," since they can be stated without using that word. However, other words, like "plank," have to be used. This is just as vague as "ship." Can we be sure that there is a range of ultimate facts that can be described without using any vague expressions at all? Such a belief would surely need very careful justification.

The second qualm is this: Identity over time, as discussed in the case of the ship, must surely be governed by principles such as this: "Replacing some, but not too many, parts of an artifact does not destroy it, but leaves you with the very same artifact." Such principles are vague. How could the identity relation, which they determine, be precise? One has an adequate understanding of vagueness only when one has resolved this question.[19]

BIBLIOGRAPHICAL NOTES

The best introductory article is Black [1937]; see also Dummett [1975].

A classic text for the supervaluation theory is Fine [1975]; for the degree theory, Goguen [1969]. For a more philosophical and less technical account of degree theory, see Peacocke [1981].

Some very important contributions to these issues have been made by Crispin Wright: See especially Wright [1975], which contains, along with much else, an argument (sketched above in section 2.1) for the utility of vagueness.

For the notion of partial belief, see Ramsey [1926] and Jeffrey [1965], chaps 3 and 4. A substantive question would be whether a similar argument could be used to underwrite objective probabilities. If the answer is affirmative, as Mellor [1971] argues, then a question of crucial importance would be whether one can give a satisfactory

---

[19] Q: How would you evaluate the following argument?

If you exist at all, you are a vague object, for we believe the following tolerance principle: A molecule more or less cannot make the difference between whether you exist or do not. On this basis, we can construct a paradoxical argument: Taking away one molecule will not make you cease to exist, taking away one more will not make you cease to exist, and so on; thus you can exist even if no molecules of you do. This shows that you are as vague as a heap. However, there are no vague objects, therefore you do not exist.

See Unger [1979].

account of why the arguments reach different destinations: degrees of truth in one case, objective probabilities in the other.

On the question raised at the very end, as to whether there are vague objects, see Evans [1978], Nathan Salmon [1982], p. 243ff, and Wiggins [1986].

3.   ACTING RATIONALLY

3.1.   NEWCOMB'S PARADOX

You are confronted with a choice. There are two boxes before you, *A* and *B*. You may either open both boxes, or else just open *B*. You may keep what is inside any box you open, but you may not keep what is inside any box you do not open. The background is this.

A very powerful being, who has been invariably accurate in his predictions about your behavior in the past, has already acted in the following way:

> He has put $1,000 in box *A*.
> If he has predicted that you will open just box *B*, he has in addition put $1,000,000 in box *B*.
> If he has predicted that you will open both boxes, he has put nothing in box *B*.

The paradox consists in the fact that there appears to be a decisive argument for the view that the most rational thing to do is to open both boxes; and also a decisive argument for the view that the most rational thing to do is to open just box *B*. The arguments commend incompatible courses of action: If you take both boxes, you cannot also take just box *B*. Putting the arguments together entails the overall conclusion that taking both boxes is the most rational thing and also not the most rational thing. This is unacceptable, yet the arguments from which it derives are apparently acceptable.

The argument for opening both boxes goes like this. The powerful being – let us call him the Predictor – has already acted. Either he has put money in both boxes or he has put money in just box *A*. In the first case, by opening both boxes you will win $1,001,000. In the second case, by opening both boxes you will at least win $1,000, which is better than nothing. By contrast, if you were to open just box *B,* you would win just $1,000,000 on the first assumption (i.e., that the Predictor has put money in both boxes) and nothing on the second assumption (i.e., that the Predictor has put money just in box *A*). In either case, you would be $1,000 worse off than had you opened both boxes. So opening both boxes is the best thing to do.

The argument for opening just box *B* goes as follows. Since the Predictor has always been right in his previous predictions, you have every reason for thinking that he will be right in this one. So you have every reason to think that if you were to open both boxes, the Predictor would have predicted this and so would have left box *B* empty. So you have every reason to think that it would not be best to open both boxes. Likewise, you have every reason to think that if you choose to open just box *B,* the Predictor will have predicted this, and so will have put $1,000,000 inside. Imagine a third party, who knows all the facts. He will bet heavily that if you open just box *B* you will win $1,000,000. He will bet heavily that if you open both boxes you will get only $1,000. You have to agree that his bets are rational. So it must be rational for you to open just box *B*.

This paradox has been used to compare two different principles for determining how it is rational to act. One principle is this: You should act so as to maximize the benefit you can expect from your action. In stating this principle, "benefit" is usually replaced by the technical term "utility." Part of the point of the technical term is to break any supposed connection between rationality and selfishness or lack of moral fiber. A benefit or "utility" consists in any situation that you want to obtain. If you are altruistic, you may desire someone else's welfare, and then an improvement in his welfare will count as a utility to you. If you want to do what is morally right, an action will attract utility simply by being in conformity with what, in your eyes, morality requires, even if from other points of view, say the purely material one, the consequences of the action are not beneficial to you.

There is obviously something appealing in the principle that it is rational to act so as to *maximize expected utility* – MEU for short. Consider gambling: The bigger the prize in the lottery, the more money it is rational to pay for a ticket, everything else being equal; the larger the number of tickets, the less money it is rational to pay. The MEU principle tells you to weigh both these factors. If there are 100 tickets and there is just one prize of $1,000, then you will think that you are doing well if you can buy a ticket for less than $10. (For consider: If you could buy them *all* for less than $10 each, then you could be certain of gaining $1,000 for an expenditure of less than $1,000.) If the tickets cost more than $10, you may have to think of the lottery as a way of raising money for a charity that you wish to support, if you are to buy a ticket.

Such an example contains a number of quite unrealistic assumptions. Some of these are inessential, but at least one is essential if the MEU principle is to compare any possible pair of actions for their degree of rationality. This is the supposition that utilities and probabilities can be measured.[1,2,3] If they can, then we can simply compute which of the actions open to us have greatest expected utility: We multiply the measure of utility by the measure of the probability of that utility accruing. Suppose that there are two lotteries, one as described above, with 1,000 tickets at $1 and a single $1,000 prize, and another with 99 tickets at $10 and a single $999 prize. The MEU principle tells you to prefer buying tickets in the second lottery rather than the first. For the first, the expected utility is the chance you think you have of winning, $\frac{1}{100}$, multiplied by the utility of the win, which can be represented as 1,000; so the expected utility is 10. For the second, it is $\frac{1}{99} \times 999 = 10.09$ (approximately).

---

[1] Q: Suppose that on Monday you are penniless and starving, but that on Tuesday you win $1,000,000 in a betting pool. Do you think that the number 5 can be used to measure the utility of $5 to you on each of these days?

[2] Q: Suppose you have four courses of action open to you, (a)–(d), associated with rewards as follows: (a) $1, (b) $6, (c) $10,000, (d) $10,005. Do you think that the number 5 can be used to measure both the difference between the utilities of (a) and (b) and the difference between the utilities of (c) and (d)?

[3] Q*: Discuss the following view:
Although people want things other than money, we can nevertheless measure how much they want things in numerical terms, by finding out how much they would be willing to pay, supposing, perhaps *per impossibile*, that what they want could be bought. If a man says he wants a happy love affair, we can measure the utility of this upshot to him by finding out how much money he would be willing to give up to get what he wants. Would he give up his car? His house? His job? All that is needed is the ability to imagine things being other than they are: to imagine that things that in fact cannot be bought can be bought.

The MEU principle does not commend you to buy a ticket in either lottery. There may well be (and one would hope that there in fact were) many alternative ways of spending your money with expected utilities higher than those associated with either lottery. The principle only tells you that *if* you are going to buy a ticket for either, it should be for the second.[4]

The notion of utility was introduced in terms of what upshot an agent wants. What someone wants sometimes means what he or she wants all things considered. If I decide to go to the dentist, then typically I want to go — that is, want to go all things considered. However, what a person wants can also mean anything to which he attaches some positive value. In this sense, it is true of me, when I freely and willingly go to the dentist, that I want not to go: Not going has the positive value of sparing time and present discomfort. If I go, it is because this want is trumped by another: I want to avoid decay, and for the sake of that benefit I am prepared to put up with the loss of time and the discomfort. The appropriate connection between utility and wanting should exploit not what an agent wants overall, but rather that to which he attaches any positive value.

The situation that gives rise to Newcomb's Paradox can be represented as shown in Figure 3.1. The expected utility of opening both boxes is calculated as follows. By the background of the problem, you regard it as very likely that the Predictor will have correctly predicted your choice. Hence if you open both boxes you must think that it is very likely that the Predictor will have predicted this and so will have put no money in box B. So the expected utility is some high ratio, call it h, measuring the likelihood of this outcome, multiplied by 1,000, measuring the utility. Analogously, the expected utility for you of opening just box B is the same high ratio, measuring the likelihood of the Predictor having correctly predicted that this is what you would do, and so having put $1,000,000 in box B, multiplied by 1,000,000, measuring the utility of that outcome. Since, whatever exactly h may be, $1,000 \times h$ is much less than $1,000,000 \times h$, MEU commends opening just box B.[5]

---

4 Q*: Could the MEU principle register a general dislike of gambling, as opposed to other ways of spending money? If so, how?

5 In more detail, the expected utility of an action is calculated as follows. First, you determine the possible outcomes O_i. Each is associated with a probability, conditional upon doing A, and a utility. The expected utility of

	the Predictor has **not** put money in B	the Predictor has **put** money in B
you open $A + B$	$1,000	$1,001,000
you open just B	$ 0	$1,000,000

Figure 3.1. Newcomb's Paradox.

The MEU principle underwrites the argument for opening just box B. To resolve the paradox, however, one would need to show what was wrong with the other argument, the argument for opening both boxes. Those who are persuaded that it is rational to open both boxes will regard the fact that the MEU principle delivers the contrary recommendation as a refutation of the principle.

One attractive feature of MEU is that it is a quite general, and independently attractive, principle. Are there any other principles of rational action that are also attractive, yet that deliver a different recommendation? There are. One example is the so-called *dominance principle* – DP for short.

---

an *outcome*, relative to an action A, is the product of its utility and its probability given A. The expected utility of an action A is the sum of the expected utilities of its outcomes relative to A:

$EU(A) = [\text{prob}(O_1/A) \, U(O_1)] + [\text{prob}(O_2/A) \, U(O_2)] + \ldots$

Here $EU(A)$ stands for the expected utility of A, $\text{prob}(O_i/A)$ for the probability of outcome O_i given A, and $U(O_i)$ for the utility of that outcome. Applied to Newcomb's Paradox, using B for the action of opening only box B, and $A\&B$ for the action of opening both boxes, we have:

$EU(B) = [\text{prob}(B \text{ is empty}/B) \, U(B \text{ is empty})] + [\text{prob}(B \text{ is full}/B) \, U(B \text{ is full})]$
$= (1 - h) \, 0 + h \, 1,000,000.$

$EU(A\&B) = [\text{prob}(B \text{ is empty}/A\&B) \, U(B \text{ is empty and } A \text{ is full})]$
$+ [\text{prob}(B \text{ is full}/A\&B) \, U(B \text{ is full and } A \text{ is full})]$
$= h \, 1,000 + [(1 - h) \, 1,001,000].$

Setting $h = 0.9$ makes $EU(B) = 900,000$ and $EU(A\&B) = 101,100$, giving a nearly ninefold advantage to taking just box B.

Here I have taken for granted the notion of the probability an agent associates with an upshot. How is this probability determined, and how analyzed? My own preference is for the pioneering account in Ramsey [1926]. However, the reader should consult Jeffrey [1965]; and, for wider applications of probability, Kyburg [1961] and Levi [1967].

According to DP, it is rational to perform an action α if it satisfies the following two conditions:

(a)   Whatever else may happen, doing α will result in your being no worse off than doing any of the other things open to you.

(b)   There is at least one possible outcome in which your having done α makes you better off than you would have been had you done any of the other things open to you.

DP has commonsensical appeal. If you follow it you will act in such a way that nothing else you could do would have resulted in your faring better, except by running the risk of your faring worse.

Figure 3.1 shows that opening both boxes satisfies DP, and that opening only box B does not. Whatever the Predictor has done, you are better off opening both boxes than opening just one. In either case, you stand to gain an extra $1,000 as compared with the other course of action open to you. Hence DP and MEU conflict: They commend opposite courses of action.

One way to diagnose Newcomb's Paradox is precisely as the manifestation of this conflict of principle. The constructive task is then to explain how the principles are to be restricted in such a way that they cease to conflict, while retaining whatever element of truth they contain.

How is the Predictor so good at predicting? Suppose it worked like this. Your choice would cause the Predictor to have made the correct prediction of it. To take this alleged possibility seriously, we have to take seriously the possibility of "backward causation": that is, a later event (here your choice) causing an earlier one (here the Predictor's prediction). Let us for the moment take this in our stride. If one knew that this was how things worked, surely there could not be two views about what it would be rational to do. One should open just box B, for this would cause the Predictor to predict that this is what one would do, which would lead to his putting $1,000,000 in box B. Not making this choice, by contrast, would lead to his not putting the $1,000,000 in box B. Clearly it would be crazy not to choose to open just box B.

The original case was, perhaps, underdescribed. Perhaps it did allow for the possibility (if there is such a possibility) of backward causation. To prevent confusion, let us stipulate that the *original case* is one that excludes backward causation. It is instructive, however, to consider this *other* case, where there is supposed to be backward causation. Perhaps the attraction of opening just box *B* in the original case sprang from thinking of it as the backward causation case. More generally, perhaps the paradox strikes us as paradoxical only to the extent that we confuse the original case with the backward causation case. To the extent that we think of the case as involving backward causation, we are tempted by MEU. To the extent that we think of it as excluding backward causation we are tempted by DP. What strikes us as conflicting views of the same case are really views of different cases.

In the original case, one might suppose that the Predictor bases his decision on general laws, together with particular past facts. These might all be physical, or they might be psychological: For example, the laws might be laws of psychology, and the particular facts might concern your personality. There is no question of backward causation. Then the basis for the prediction consists in facts that lie in the past. Rejecting backward causation, this means that nothing you can now do can affect the basis for the prediction. Hence nothing you now do can make any difference to whether there is or is not money in box *B*. So you should open both boxes.

There is a complicating factor: Suppose that determinism is true. Suppose, in particular, that the psychological laws, together with data about your character up to the time at which the Predictor made his prediction, determine how you will now act, in the sense of making it impossible for you to do anything other than what, in fact, you will do. This may totally undermine the idea of rational decision, and so make the whole question of what is best to do one that cannot arise. In short, there is a case for saying that if there were such a Predictor, then there could be no question about which choice is rational. I shall ignore this case, and argue that it is rational to open both boxes. Those who are moved by it could read my conclusion as hypothetical: If we can make sense of rationality at all in the Newcomb situation, then the rational thing is to open both boxes.[6]

---

[6]   If you think that the arguments for one-boxing and for two-boxing are equally compelling, then you could see this as refuting the story (as in the case of the Barber). That is, you could see the unacceptable consequence as showing that there could not be a being capable of predicting free choices. For this line, see Schlesinger [1974b]. See also a critical discussion by Benditt and Ross [1976], which makes some important distinctions.

In defending this conclusion, I need to consider whether, as claimed earlier, it is rational for the onlookers to bet heavily on the following two conditionals:

(a)   if you select both boxes, box *B* will be empty.
(b)   if you select just box *B,* it will contain $1,000,000.

If they are rational, the onlookers will bet in accordance with their expectations. Their expectations are the same as yours. They have very strong reason to believe the two conditionals, given the Predictor's past successes. How can this be reconciled with my claim that if the Predictor bases his prediction on past evidence, then it is rational to open both boxes? If it is rational for the onlookers to expect the conditionals to be true, it must be rational for you to expect the same. However, it seems, you have a *choice* about which conditional will count. It is rational, surely, to make the second conditional count, and you can do this by opening just box *B*. How can one reconcile the rationality of belief in the conditionals with the rationality of opening both boxes?

Let us look more closely at the basis of the rationality of belief in the conditionals. We can do this by looking at it from the point of view of the onlookers. They reason as follows. The Predictor has always been right in the past. Since he has already filled the boxes, his prediction is based on knowing some past facts about you and your circumstances, and applying some generalizations. Our best evidence for what he has predicted is what you choose to do. This is why we believe the conditionals. Your opening just box *B* is evidence that the Predictor has predicted this and, hence, by the way the problem is set up, is evidence that he has filled box *B* with $1,000,000. Likewise for the other possibility.

The rationality of these beliefs does not entail the rationality of opening just box *B*   This is most easily seen if we switch to the subject's point of view: to *your* point of view, as we are pretending. The Predictor makes his choice on the basis of past facts about you, together with some generalizations. To simplify, let us say that there are two relevant possible facts about what sort of person you were at the time the Predictor made his prediction: Either you were a one-boxer – that is, a person disposed to open just box *B* – or you were a two-boxer – that is, a person disposed to open both boxes. Now if you find a tendency to open both boxes well up in you, that is bad news.[7] It is evidence that you are now a two-boxer and, all other things being equal, is thereby evidence that you were a two-boxer at the time when the Predictor made his decision. Hence it is evidence that he will have predicted that you will open both boxes, and so it is evidence that there will be no money in the *B* box. However, there is no point in trying to extirpate this disposition, and it would be a confusion to think that you could make any difference to the situation by resisting it. There is no point trying to extirpate it *now,* since either the Predictor has made his prediction on the basis of perceiving such a disposition in you or he has not; and getting rid of it now, supposing it has been perceived, is closing the stable door after the horse has bolted. It would be a confusion to think that anything you can now do can make any difference as to whether or not you were a two-boxer at the time the Predictor made his prediction. If you found in yourself an inclination to open just box *B,* that would be good news, for analogous reasons; but it is an inclination that it would be more prudent to resist. By resisting it and opening both boxes, you cannot make the money that you can reasonably presume is already in the *B* box go away, and you will gain the extra $1,000 in the *A* box.

Here is an objection. If this is where the reasoning were to end, would not a really good Predictor have predicted this, and therefore have ensured that there is nothing in box *B*? Furthermore, had you taken the reasoning through a further twist, using the fact just mentioned as a reason for in the end taking just box *B,* the Predictor would have predicted this too, and so would have filled box *B*. So is not this what you should do?

However, the original difficulty remains and cannot be overcome. No matter what twists and turns of reasoning you go in for now, you cannot affect what the Predictor has already done. Even if you could make yourself now into a one-boxer, it would not help. What mattered was whether you were a one-boxer, or a person likely to become a

---

[7]   **Q:** How would you respond to the following argument?

It would come as wonderful news to learn that I am a one-boxer, for then I will be able to infer that I will soon be rich. However, I can give myself that news simply by deciding to be a one-boxer. So this is what I should decide to do.

one-boxer, at the time when the Predictor made his prediction. You cannot change the past.[8,9]

We have said that the Predictor has *always* been right in the past.[10] Let us imagine, in particular, that he has always been right about Newcomb problems. We shall suppose that each person is confronted with the problem only once in his life (there is no second chance), and that the Predictor has never been wrong: That is, never has a two-boxer found anything in box *B,* and never has a one-boxer found box *B* empty. Most of your friends have already had the chance. The one-boxers among them are now millionaires. You wish above all things that you were a millionaire like them, and now your chance has come: You are faced with the Newcomb problem. Is it not true that all you have to do is choose just box *B*? Is that not a sure-fire way to riches? So how could it be rational to refuse it?

So far, this raises no new considerations: The two-boxer's reply still stands. However, I have put the matter this way in order to add the following twist. Being of good two-box views, you think that the Predictor is, for some crazy reason, simply rewarding irrationality: He makes one-boxers rich, and one-boxers are irrational. Still, if you want to be rich above all things, then is not the *rational* thing to do to join the irrational people in opening just box *B*? Sir John Harington (1561–1612) wrote that

> Treason doth never prosper; what's the reason?
> Why, if it prosper, none dare call it treason.

Likewise, if "irrationality" pays, then it is not irrationality at all! You

---

[8] Q: We have envisaged the choice before you being a once-in-a-lifetime chance. However, suppose you knew that you were going to be allowed to make this choice once a week for the rest of your life, and suppose the facts about the Predictor remain the same. What is the most rational policy to pursue?

[9] Q: Consider a variant of the problem – let us call it the "sequential Newcomb." The difference is that you are allowed to make your choice in two stages: You can elect to open box *B*, reserving your choice about box *A* until you find out what is in box *B*. Suppose you open *B* and there is nothing inside. Should you elect also to open *A*? Suppose you open *B* and there is $1,000,000 inside. Should you elect also to open *A*? Do your answers have any implications for the original Newcomb?

[10] Q: Consider a variant in which he has *mostly* been right in the past. Would this make any difference to the argument? Try working out what the MEU commends if we set the probability of the Predictor being right at 0.6.

want to be rich like your millionaire friends, and if you think as they do you will be. It is rational to adapt means to ends, so it is rational to think the way they think.

This suggestion can be represented as involving two main points. The first is that one might reasonably want to be a different sort of person from the sort one is: here, a less rational sort. Some people committed to lucidity and truth as values find this suggestion unpalatable.[11] However, a second point is needed: that if it is reasonable to want to be a different sort of person, then it is reasonable, even as things are, to act as that other sort of person would have acted. The second point is what secures the passage from envying the one-boxers to the claim that it would be rational to follow their lead. Once clearly stated, this second point can be seen to be incorrect: Given that you are not a "natural" one-boxer, given that you are persuaded by the argument for two-boxing, nothing can as things stand make it *rational* for you to one-box.[12]

A clear perception of the advantages of being a one-boxer cannot give you a *reason* for becoming one – even if that were in your power. An atheist might clearly perceive the comfort to be derived from theism, but this does not give him or her a *reason* for believing that God exists. The light of reason cannot direct one toward what one perceives as irrational. To adopt a position one regards as irrational one needs to rely on something other than reason: drugs, fasting, chanting, dancing, or whatever.

This way of dealing with the paradox takes no account of the two principles, MEU and DP. Is either to be accepted? MEU cannot be correct, since it commends taking just box *B*. DP cannot be correct since, in the other version of the paradox, in which backward causation was admitted, DP wrongly commended taking both

---

[11] Q: What are your own views on this point? Some people say that they wish they could believe in life after death. If this wish involves wishing that they could cease to be moved by the evidence *against* life after death, it is an example of the sort of desire whose reasonableness or rationality is in question.

[12] Human frailty being what it is, no doubt social pressures would, in the envisaged circumstances, make one-boxers of all but the stoutest of us. This does not touch the question of what the *rational* course of action in such circumstances would be.

boxes.[13,14] However, we may be able to see why the principles let us down when they did, and this may lead to ways of suitably restricting them.

In the backward causation case, it is no accident that DP gives the wrong result. It has no means of taking into account the fact that your choice will affect what is in the boxes, by affecting the Predictor. More generally, it gives the wrong result because it makes no provision for the ways in which one's acting can affect the probabilities of outcomes. The backward causation case alone shows that DP cannot serve as it stands as a correct principle of rational action: It cannot be rational to act in such a way as to cause a diminution in the likelihood of someone else doing something that would increase one's benefits.

Equally, it is no accident that MEU gives the right result for the backward causation case. The rationale of MEU is given by the thought that it is rational to act in ways one takes to be likely to *promote* one's benefits. In the backward causation case, one has reason to believe that how one acts will affect one's benefits by affecting the Predictor's decision. In this case, the conditional probabilities reflect the probability of one's action genuinely promoting one rather than another outcome.

By contrast, in the original case, this does not hold. The conditional probabilities obtain, but in a way that fails to reflect the underlying rationale of the MEU. The probability that if you open both boxes, box *B* will be empty is indeed high; but it is not high because your opening both boxes will have any causal role in bringing it about

---

13
    Q: Consider some familiar gambling game (e.g., roulette or poker). Can DP be used to say which bets in your selected game are rational? Assume that the only aim is to win as much money as possible.

14
    Q: Israel is wondering whether to withdraw from territories it occupies. Egypt is wondering whether or not to go to war with Israel. From Israel's point of view, the utilities are as follows:

	Egypt declares war	Egypt does not declare war
Israel withdraws	0	2
Israel remains	1	3

Show how this example can be used to demonstrate that DP does not always give correct results. (See Bar-Hillel and Margalit [1972].)

that box B is empty. The right restriction on MEU, so far as New-comb's Paradox goes, is that one should act on the principle only when the conditional probabilities reflect what one believes one's actions will *produce*.[15]

We have seen that DP is not an acceptable principle of rational action, since it takes no account of conditional probabilities. This fact explains why it happens to give the right result in the original case. Here, because the probabilities are irrelevant, in that they do not reflect the likely effects of the possible actions, it is right to ignore them. So far as this case goes, the appropriate restriction on DP is that it can be used only when there is no relevant difference in the probability of the various possible outcomes.

Though these considerations explain away Newcomb's Paradox, they leave a great deal of work to be done within the wider task of understanding the nature of rational action. A first point to consider would be whether the modified versions of MEU and DP are *consistent:* whether, that is, they would deliver the same account for all cases of how it is rational to act.[16] One would have to go on to ask

---

[15] One could capture this by saying that the relevant probability, for a correct MEU, is not the conditional probability of an outcome upon an action, but rather the unconditional probability of a statement of the form "If I were to act thus, this would be the outcome." This so-called counterfactual conditional requires for its truth something approaching the relation between act and upshot mentioned in the text: The act should *produce* the upshot. Compare Gibbard and Harper [1978].

[16] Q: How would you respond to the following argument?
The dominance principle DP cannot conflict with the MEU principle, if by this is meant that there is a situation in which an action with maximum expected utility would fail to be preferred by the dominance principle. For any upshot, the probability of its occurring is the same regardless of the action, so the only relevant fact, for each upshot, is the utility. So MEU and DP cannot diverge. The table makes this plain:

	P_1	P_2
A_1	5	2
A_2	4	2

A_1 and A_2 are actions open to you. The possible outcomes are P_1 and P_2. If you do A_1 and P_1 is the outcome, your utility is measured by the number 5. Likewise for the other cells in the table. The dominance principle commends A_1 in preference to A_2. The MEU either does likewise or else is indifferent between A_1 and A_2, and in either case the principles do

whether they are *correct:* whether either delivers for all cases a correct account of how it is rational to act. It is unlikely that any such simple principles would be adequate to this task. Indeed, many philosophers are skeptical concerning many of the notions upon which this discussion has been based. It is not at all plausible to think that the values that are at issue in deciding what to do are measurable in the way that has been presupposed. It would be important to consider whether any substantive principles of rationality can be formulated that do not rest on this supposition. A wider issue is whether we have any right to a supposedly objective, culture-independent notion of rationality as a scale against which any action at all can be measured. Perhaps there are species of rationality, or perhaps rationality is simply one value among others. In the next section, I consider one alleged threat to the coherence of the notion of rationality.

3.2.   THE PRISONER'S DILEMMA

You and I have been arrested for drug running and placed in separate cells. Each of us learns, through his own attorney, that the district attorney has resolved as follows (and we have every reason to trust this information):

1.   If we both remain silent, the district attorney will have to drop the drug-running charge for lack of evidence, and will instead charge us with the much more minor offense of possessing dangerous weapons: We would then each get a year in jail.
2.   If we both confess, we shall both get five years in jail.
3.   If one remains silent and the other confesses, the one who confesses will get off scot-free (for turning State's evidence), and the other will go to jail for ten years.
4.   The other prisoner is also being told all of (1)–(4).

How is it rational to act? We build into the story the following further features:

---

not conflict. To show this, let us call the agent's probabilities of P_1 and P_2 respectively π_1 and π_2. We do not know what these values are, but we can be sure that $5 \times \pi_1$ is greater than $4 \times \pi_1$, and that $2 \times \pi_2$ is not greater than $2 \times \pi_2$. So MEU must either commend A_1 or else be neutral.

	you confess	you don't confess
I confess	‹5,5›	‹0,10›
I don't confess	‹10,0›	‹1,1›

Figure 3.2. The Prisoner's Dilemma.

5.　　Each is concerned only with getting the smallest sentence for himself.

6.　　Neither has any information about the likely behavior of the other, except that (5) holds of him and that he is a rational agent.

There is an obvious line of reasoning in favor of confessing. It is simply that whatever you do, I shall do better to confess. For if you remain silent and I confess, I shall get what I most want, no sentence at all; whereas if you confess, then I shall do much better by confessing too (five years) than by remaining silent (ten years). We can represent the situation by Figure 3.2, and the reasoning in favor of confessing is the familiar dominance principle (DP).

In the figure <0,10> represents the fact that on this option I go to prison for zero years, and you go for ten years; and so on. The smaller the number on my (left) side of the pair, the better I am pleased. It is easy to see that confessing dominates silence: Confessing, as compared to silence, saves me five needless years if you confess, and one if you do not.

Since you and I are in relevantly similar positions, and [by (6)] we are both rational, presumably we shall reason in the same way, and thus perform the same action. So if it is rational for me to confess, it is rational for you to do likewise; but then we shall each go to prison for five years. If we both remain silent, we would go to prison for only one year each. By acting supposedly rationally, we shall, it seems, secure for ourselves an outcome that is worse for both of us than what we could achieve.

On this view, rational action in some circumstances leads to worse outcomes than other courses of action. Even if this is depressing, it is not as it stands paradoxical: We all know that irrational gambles can succeed. What is arguably paradoxical is that the case is one in which the failure of rationality to produce the best results is not a matter of some chance intervention, but is a predictable and inevitable consequence of so-called rational reasoning. How, in that case, can it be rational to be "rational"?[17] The allegedly unacceptable consequence of the apparently acceptable reasoning is that rational action can be seen in advance to make a worse outcome highly likely.

If this is a paradox, then the correct response, I believe, is to deny that the consequence is really unacceptable. The unacceptability is supposed to consist in the fact that if we were both to act in a certain way, we would be better off than if each were to follow the supposed dictates of rationality. Hence rationality is not the *best* guide to how to act, in that acting in the other way would lead to a better outcome for both. The trouble with this suggestion is that any guide to action has to be available to the agent's decision-making processes. To be guided by the thought that we would both be better off if both remained silent than if both confessed, I would need to know that you would remain silent. What it is rational to do must be relative to what we know. If we are ignorant, then of course acting rationally may not lead us to the best upshot. Here, the ignorance of each concerns what the other will do; and this, rather than some defect in rationality, is what yields the less than optimal upshot.

However, we are now close to a paradox of a different sort. I have said that there is a compelling argument for the rationality of confessing. However, it appears that there is also a strong case for the rationality of remaining silent. If this case is good, then two apparently acceptable arguments lead to conclusions that, taken together, are unacceptable.

The argument for silence goes like this. We both know we are rational agents, because that is built into the story. We therefore know that any reason one of us has for acting will apply to the other. Hence we know that we shall do the same thing. There are two courses of action that count as doing the same thing: both confessing or both remaining silent. Of these, the latter is preferable for both of us. So of the available courses of action, it is obvious which each of us must rationally prefer: remaining silent. This, then, is the rational choice.

This argument invites a revenge. Suppose silence is the rational choice, and that I know it is. Then, in knowing that you are rational,

---

[17]   Compare: How could it be rational to be a two-boxer, if being a one-boxer would ensure that one would be a millionaire?

I know that it is the choice you will make. So I know that you will remain silent. However, in that case it must be rational for me to confess, thus securing my preferred outcome: getting off scot-free. On the other hand, I know that you can reason like this too; therefore you, if rational, will not keep silent. In that case it is again – but more urgently – rational for me to confess. The way of silence is unstable. Thus the hypothesis that keeping silent is the rational choice is refuted.

This shows that the Prisoner's Dilemma does not really entail an unacceptable conclusion concerning rationality. We should not, however, be content with simply showing this: We should see how the case connects with the principles of rational action already discussed.

The MEU principle, as stated in section 3.1, claimed that the rational act was whatever maximized expected utility, where this was to be understood in terms of two factors: the desirability of a certain outcome and its probability, conditional upon the performance of a given act. In connection with Newcomb's Paradox, I originally said that the relevant probabilities were

(a)   the probability of there being $1,000,000 in box B, *given that* I choose to open both boxes, and

(b)   the probabilty of there being $1,000,000 in box B, *given that* I choose to open just box B.

In the discussion, I claimed that these are not the right probabilities to consider in those cases in which these conditional probabilities do not reflect the tendency of my action to *produce* the outcome in question. So what are the right probabilties to consider? One suggestion is that they are

(a´)   the probability of my bringing it about that there will be $1,000,000 in box B by choosing both boxes, and

(b´)   the probability of my bringing it about that there will be $1,000,000 in box B by choosing one box.

Both of these probabilities are 0. If we stipulate that anything known to be true anyway (having a probability of 1, regardless of my action) is something that *anything* I do counts as bringing about, then opening box A has an expected utility equal to the utility of $1,000, and opening only box B has an expected utility of 0. The version of MEU that considers the probabilities (a´) and (b´), rather than (a) and (b), supports two-boxing.

Let us apply the contrast between these two versions of MEU to the Prisoner's Dilemma, starting with the original version. The probability of you confessing, given that I confess, is high and equal to the probability of you remaining silent, given that I remain silent. Moreover, the probability of you confessing, given that I remain silent, is low, and so is the probability of the converse. These conditional probabilities follow from my knowledge, built in to the example, that you and I will reason in similar ways, since we are both rational.[18] With suitable utilities, there will be versions of the dilemma in which MEU, in its original form, designates silence as the rational course of action.[19]

In its modifed form, MEU was to take into account the probability of an action *producing* the relevant outcome. Since that probability is by stipulation 0 in the present case, because each of us makes his decision before knowing what the other has decided, the modified MEU does not give us any guidance: All the expected utilities, understood in this way, are the same. However, this fact would be a telling reason for applying DP: If you have no idea what outcomes your actions will bring about, choose that action that will make things better for you whatever the other person does.

It has been suggested that Newcomb's Paradox is simply a version of the Prisoner's Dilemma. In Newcomb's Paradox, the crucial matter – whether or not there is anything in box *B* – is one of match: The money is in the box if and only if my action matches the "prediction." It does not matter whether the "prediction" occurs before or after the act of choice; what matters is that the act of choice should have no effect on the content of the prediction. Likewise, match is of the essence in the Prisoner's Dilemma: Knowing that we are both rational, I expect my action to match yours, just as I expect the prediction to match my choice. Moreover, just as I cannot affect the prediction, so I cannot affect your choice. Figure 3.3 sets out the similarities.

---

[18] Q: Clarify the assumption behind the remark that if two people are rational, then for any problem both will reason about it in similar ways. Is the assumption justifiable?

[19] Q: Using the numbers in the table in the text as the utilities of the various outcomes (prefix each with a minus sign to show that the outcomes are mostly undesirable), how could you assign conditional probabilities (using numbers between 0 and 1) in such a way as to make the expected utility of silence higher than that of confession? [For details, you may find it useful to refer to footnote 5 above.]   Your assignment will justify the sentence in the text.

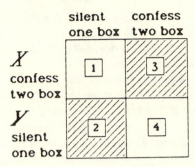

Figure 3.3. Similarities between Newcomb's Paradox and the Prisoner's Dilemma. I have to choose whether to do X (confess, take both boxes) or Y (remain silent, take just one box). The column indicates what the other character in the story may do: The other prisoner remains silent or confesses; the Predictor predicts that I shall one-box or else that I shall two-box. My preferences among the outcomes, from best to worst, are in this order: 1, 2, 3, 4. The "matching possibilities" are shaded: The other prisoner does what I do, the Predictor predicts correctly. I know that my choice cannot affect whether or not a match will occur. I know that a match is much more likely than a mismatch.

In a nutshell, the two arguments we have considered are these:

A.   Do X, since you are better off, whatever the other does, than you would be if you were to do Y: 1 is better than 2, and 3 is better than 4.
B.   Do Y, since match is the most likely kind of outcome, and of these 2 is better than 3.

If this analogy is correct, then one has *consistent* views on the problems only if one is either a two-boxer and a believer in confessing, or else a one-boxer and a believer in silence. My view is the first.
The Prisoner's Dilemma is a simplified version of a well-known conflict: If our cooperating means each of us forgoing something that he (or she) would otherwise have preferred, then cooperation appears not to be in my best interests. What serves my purposes best is to secure cooperation from you, while not being cooperative in return. In the Prisoner's Dilemma, what would be best for me is that you remain silent, perhaps under the influence of persuasion, threats, or promises from me, while I, perhaps reneging on undertakings to you, confess.

If the first view is correct, and X-ing is the rational thing to do, then if we both pursue our interests rationally, we shall end up serving these interests less well then we might. This is not really unacceptable, for it is true; but it may seem depressing.

In the case we have considered, there is just a single situation requiring a decision. Suppose instead that we are confronted with a "multiple Prisoner's Dilemma": Suppose that there are a series of choices, and that we each know this – in particular, we each know that this is not the last time we shall be playing the game with each other – and that we also know that the other will remember, and no doubt be guided by, what has happened on previous occasions. There is an argument to the effect that this new situation would push me in the direction of silence. Suppose you get the idea that I am the sort of person who generally confesses. Then I know that this will make you confess too, to protect yourself from the disasterous consequences of silence, and the overall result will be less than the best for me, time after time. So I have an interest in getting you to believe that I am the sort of person who generally remains silent. One way I can propagate this view is by in fact remaining silent. (We all know, from our knowledge of used car salesmen and politicians, that this is not the only way to try to achieve this kind of effect.) I also know that you will follow the same policy. So in this situation the cooperative policy of silence would appear to be the rational one.[20]

There is fascinating evidence that this is not far from the truth. In some computer simulations of Prisoner's Dilemma situations, the following strategy did better than any other: Start by remaining silent; thereafter do what the other player did during the previous round. In suitable circumstances, this will lead to a situation of stable cooperation. Since the multiple Prisoner's Dilemma corresponds more closely to more of real life than the single case, it may be that the upshot of the discussion ought not to be so depressing: Perhaps rational self-interest is not doomed to lead to a nonoptimal outcome. However, the main point that I have been concerned to establish is that the paradoxical appearance of the Prisoner's Dilemma, like that of Newcomb's Paradox, can be resolved.

---

[20]   Q*: Suppose, however, that all parties know in advance how many times they will be in this situation – fifty times, say. How would you state the case for the view that the most rational policy is always to confess?

BIBLIOGRAPHICAL NOTES

Newcomb's Paradox (also known as Newcomb's Problem) first appeared in print in Nozick [1969]. Nozick says that the paradox was invented by Dr William Newcomb of the Livermore Radiation Laboratories in California. As far as I know, Newcomb himself has not written about his paradox.

The discussions to which I am most indebted are Mackie [1977] and Gibbard and Harper [1978]. For a defense of one-boxing see Bar-Hillel and Margalit [1972].

For a systematic study of rational decision see Jeffrey [1965]. For an introduction to probability, see Black [1967].

A very good overview of Newcomb's Paradox and the Prisoner's Dilemma is provided by Campbell [1985], in an introduction to an excellent collection of essays on these topics.

The issues raised by the Prisoner's Dilemma connect closely with practical problems. Parfit [1984], chaps 2–4, stresses these in the course of his immensely stimulating discussion.

For the similarity between Newcomb's Paradox and the Prisoner's Dilemma see Lewis [1979]. For a similar problem, see Selton [1978].

For an account of the results of computer simulation of various strategies for playing multiple Prisoner's Dilemma games, see Axelrod [1984].

4.   BELIEVING RATIONALLY

This chapter concerns problems about what it is to have knowledge or rational belief. It is in two main sections: The first, called "Paradoxes of Confirmation," is about two paradoxes that might be called "philosophers' paradoxes." Let me explain.

Most of the paradoxes in this book are quite straightforward to state. Seeing what is paradoxical about them does not require any special knowledge – you do not have to be a games theorist or a statistician to see what is paradoxical about Newcomb's Paradox or the Prisoner's Dilemma, nor do you have to be a physicist or sportsman to see what is paradoxical about Zeno's paradoxes. By contrast, the paradoxes of confirmation arise, and can only be understood, in the context of a specifically philosophical project. Therefore these paradoxes need some background (section 4.1.1) before being introduced (in sections 4.1.2 and 4.1.3). The background section sets out the nature of the project within which the paradoxes arise.

The second main section of the chapter concerns the paradox of the Unexpected Examination. Although it is hard to resolve, it is easy enough to state. This paradox has been used to cast doubt on intuitively natural principles about rational belief and knowledge.

4.1.   PARADOXES OF CONFIRMATION

4.1.1.   Background

We all believe that there is a firm distinction between strong, good, or reliable evidence on the one hand, and weak, bad, or unreliable evidence on the other. If a stranger at the racetrack tells you that Wolf-face will win the next race, and you have no other relevant information, you would be a fool to bet heavily on Wolf-face. The evidence that he will win is extremely thin. However, had the trainer

73

given you the same tip, that would have provided you with much stronger evidence. It would be stronger still if you knew that the trainer was a crook who believed that you were on to him, and if you also knew that he thought a good tip would buy you off.

Most of our actions are guided by scarcely conscious assessments of how good our evidence is for certain of our beliefs. When we choose what film to see or what restaurant to patronize we are often guided by past experience: by whether the director or actors have good track records, or whether the restaurant has produced good food in the past. We are also guided by what other people say: We weigh their testimony, trusting some – good reviewers, or people we know to be good judges of food – more than others. In such everyday cases, our assessment of the quality of the evidence is pretty rough and ready: We recognize good judges and bad judges, good signs and bad signs; but we never normally ask ourselves what *constitutes* a good judge or a good sign.

The philosophical project within which the paradoxes of section 4.1 arise is to state general principles determining what counts as good evidence. Such principles sometimes surface outside philosophy departments. In law courts, for example, explicit categorizations of the evidence ("circumstantial," "inadmissible") are used to grade it; and in scientific investigations, in particular those involving certain kinds of numerically structured data, there are elaborate and sophisticated statistical theories bearing on the question of the extent to which data support a hypothesis.

The branch of philosophy in which philosophers have tried to articulate general principles determining the quality of evidence is called "confirmation theory." These attempts have given rise to surprising paradoxes. Understanding them will lead to a better idea of the nature of evidence.

If a body of propositions constitutes *some* evidence (however slight) for a hypothesis, let us say that these propositions *confirm* the hypothesis. From this starting point one might hope to develop an account of what one should believe. For example, one might think that one ought to believe, of all the relevant hypotheses that one can conceive, that which is best confirmed by all of one's data. Be that as it may, there are problems enough even with the starting point, let alone what one might develop from it.

A very natural thought is that the following principle will play some fundamental role in an account of confirmation:

G1. A generalization is confirmed by any of its instances.

Here are some examples of generalizations:

1. All emeralds are green.
2. Whenever the price of cocaine falls, its consumption rises.
3. Everyone I have spoken to this morning thinks that the Democrats will win the next election.
4. All AIDS victims have such-and-such a chromosome.

G1 asserts that these propositions are confirmed by their instances – that is, respectively, by this, that, or the other emerald being green; by cases in which the price of cocaine falls and its consumption increases; by the fact that I spoke to Mary this morning, and she thinks that the Democrats will win; and by the fact that Frank, who has AIDS, also has this chromosome. Notice that G1 does not assert, crazily, that an instance can *establish* a generalization. A single instance can *confirm*, according to G1, but obviously that does not settle the matter. A single instance does not even show that it is rational to believe the hypothesis, let alone that it is true.

I have spoken both of objects (like emeralds) and of facts (like the fact that Frank has AIDS and also this chromosome) as instances of generalizations, and I shall continue to do so. However, on state occasions I shall say that an instance of a generalization is itself a proposition. When the generalization has the form

All *A*'s are *B*'s,

an *instance* of it is any proposition of the form

This *A* is a *B*.

Thus

This emerald is green

is an instance of

All emeralds are green.

A *counterinstance* of a generalization "All *A*'s are *B*'s" is a proposition of the form

This *A* is not a *B*.

So

This emerald is not green

is a counterinstance of "All emeralds are green." Just as we may, on nonstate occasions, speak of green emeralds as instances of this latter proposition, so we can speak of nongreen emeralds as counterinstances of it.

The opposite of confirmation is *disconfirmation*. A hypothesis is disconfirmed by propositions that tend to show it to be false. An extreme case is *falsification:* A generalization is falsified by any counterinstance of it.

The principle G1 is to be understood to mean that any proposition that is an instance of a generalization confirms that generalization. It is not always clear how this is meant to link up with the notion of good evidence. Obviously, one AIDS victim with a certain chromosome does not alone constitute good evidence for the hypothesis that all AIDS victims have it; but perhaps a large number of instances, and no counterinstances, do add up to good evidence. If so, we shall think of each instance as making a positive contribution to this good evidence, and this is what people have in mind by the notion of confirmation. G1 does not say, absurdly, that an instance of a generalization would, in and of itself, give us good reason to believe that generalization. Rather, it says that an instance makes a positive contribution, however slight, and however liable to be outweighed by other factors, toward constituting good evidence. The idea is that if we know of an instance of a generalization, we have taken one small step toward having good evidence for that generalization, even though other things we know may undermine this evidence. Indeed, our other knowledge might include a counterinstance of that same generalization.

The quality of evidence is a matter of degree: Some evidence is stronger, other evidence weaker. One way we might try to build toward this from the idea of confirmation, together with G1, is by saying that your evidence for a generalization is stronger the more instances of it your total body of knowledge contains – provided that it contains no counterinstances. However, one must beware of supposing that it is at all easy to arrive at a correct account. The following shows that what has just been suggested is indeed wrong. One could well have come across many instances, and no counterinstances, of the generalization

All places fail to contain my spectacles

(one has searched high and low without success); yet one would be quite right to be certain that this generalization is false.

The appeal of G1 comes in part from the thought that *extrapolation* is reasonable. If all the things of kind *A* that you have examined have also been of kind *B,* then you have some reason to extrapolate to the hypothesis that all things of kind *A* are of kind *B.* Of course, the evidence may be slight, and it may be outweighed by other evidence.

We are not usually interested in confirmation (in the technical sense used here) in cases of generalizations such as "Everyone I met this morning said that the Democrats would win." If I had met a reasonably small number of people, I might say in the afternoon: "I don't need evidence – I already *know* that it's true." The idea is that my own experience already determines the truth of the generalization. The contrast is with generalizations such as "Whenever the price of cocaine falls, its consumption increases." You may know that this has held so far, but this does not settle that the proposition is true, for it speaks to future cases as well as past ones. This is the sort of generalization for which we feel we need evidence: a generalization not all of whose instances one has encountered.[1]

Inductive reasoning, as philosophers call it, consists in arguing from evidence or data to hypotheses not entailed by these data. One traditional philosophical problem has been to justify this process: to show that it is at least sometimes legitimate to "go beyond the data." Let us call this the problem of *justification.* Another philosophical problem is this: to give a general account of the kinds of inductive reasoning we *take* to be legitimate (without necessarily pronouncing on whether or not they are really legitimate). Let us call this the problem of *characterization.* We take it that it is legitimate to argue from the fact that the sun has risen every day so far to the conclusion that it will, probably, rise every day in the future; or, at least, to the conclusion that it will, probably, rise tomorrow. By contrast, we do not think that it is legitimate to argue from these same data to the conclusion that the sun will sometime cease to rise, or to the conclusion that it will not rise tomorrow.[2] The problem of characterization is to give an illuminating general account of the features of evidence that make us

---

[1]   Q: There are generalizations of which one could not be sure that one had encountered all the instances. What are some examples?

[2]   Q: Victims of the so-called Monte Carlo fallacy dispute this. They hold that the longer the run of successive reds on a fair roulette wheel the *less* likely it is that red will come up on the next spin. What, if anything, is wrong with this view? Is there anything right about it?

count it as *good* evidence, as a legitimate basis for the hypothesis in question.

An initial answer to the problem of characterization is that inductive reasoning is generally taken to be legitimate when it is a case of extrapolation: when one reasons on the assumption that what one has not experienced will resemble what one has. G1 is connected with this initial suggestion, for it specifies a way of extrapolating.

These problems of induction are akin to problems already encountered. Earlier, we asked, "Under what conditions are data good evidence for a hypothesis?" If we can answer this question in some illuminating way (and not merely by saying, for example, "When they are"), we shall thereby be close to having solved the problem of justification – for we shall then be close to showing that it *is* sometimes legitimate to go beyond the data.[3] Moreover, if we could answer the question "Under what conditions are data *taken to be* good evidence for a hypothesis?", we would have answered the problem of characterization.

We shall be concerned only with the characterization problem: not the question of whether there is any genuinely legitimate inductive reasoning, but rather the question of what sort of inductive reasoning we (rightly or wrongly) take to be legitimate. Though this seems the easier problem, attempts to answer it lead quickly to contradictions.

4.1.2.   *The Paradox of the Ravens*

Despite the initial appeal of G1, it leads, in conjunction with other apparently innocuous principles, to a paradox discovered by Carl Hempel [1945], and now generally known as the Paradox of the Ravens.

In order to derive the paradoxical consequence, we need just one other principle:

E1. If two hypotheses can be known *a priori* to be equivalent, then any data that confirm one confirm the other.

---

[3]   **Q*:** How might answering this question fail to show that inductive reasoning is sometimes legitimate, and thus fail to be a complete answer to the problem of justification?

This needs some explanation.[4] Something can be known *a priori* if it can be known without any appeal to experience. For example, one does not have to conduct any kind of social survey to discover that all women are women: Indeed, one could not discover this by a survey. What can be known *a priori* can be known simply on the basis of reflection and reasoning.

Two hypotheses are equivalent just on condition that if either one is true, so is the other, and if either one is false, so is the other. E1 asks us to consider cases in which two hypotheses can be known *a priori* to be equivalent. An example would be the hypotheses

R1. All ravens are black

and

There are no ravens that are not black

and also

R2. Everything nonblack is a nonraven.

Any two of these three hypotheses are equivalent, and this can be shown simply by reflection, without appeal to experience; so the equivalence can be known *a priori*. For example, suppose R1 is true: All ravens are black. Then, clearly, any nonblack thing is not a raven, or, as R2 puts it, is a nonraven. So if R1 is true, so is R2. Now suppose that R1 is false; then some ravens are not black. However, this means that some things that are not black are ravens, so R2

---

4   I should note a departure from Hempel's formulation – and his is the formulation used in almost all discussions. The equivalence relation he uses is that of *logical* equivalence, not *a priori* equivalence. Two propositions are logically equivalent just on condition that some system of formal logical has a theorem saying that either both propositions are true, or else both are false. Thus "Tom is a bachelor" and "Tom is a bachelor or the earth is round or not-round" are logically equivalent, but "Tom is a bachelor" and "Tom is an unmarried man" are not logically equivalent (though they can be known *a priori* to be equivalent). The intuitive motivation for the equivalence principle is this, in my view: If *P* and *Q* are in the appropriate sense equivalent, then if we can find evidence supporting *P,* we need no further empirical data to see that *Q* is thereby supported to the same extent. If this motivation is accepted, it seems clear that the appropriate equivalence relation is wider than logical equivalence, and is, precisely, *a priori* equivalence.

is false, too. Thus R1 and R2 are equivalent, and this can be known *a priori*.[5]

We can now show how the Paradox of the Ravens is derived from G1 and E1. By G1, R2 is confirmed by its instances – for example, by a white shoe, or (using the state-occasion notion of an instance) by, for example:

P1. This nonblack (in fact, white) thing is a nonraven (in fact, a shoe).

Instance P1 confirms R2, but R2 can be known *a priori* to be equivalent to R1. So, by E1, P1 confirms R1, "All ravens are black." This, on the face of it, is absurd. Data relevant to whether or not all ravens are black must be data about ravens. The color of shoes can have no bearing whatsoever on the matter. Thus G1 and E1 – apparently acceptable principles – lead to the apparently unacceptable conclusion that a white shoe confirms the hypothesis that all ravens are black. This, finally, is our paradox.

The principles of reasoning involved do not appear to be open to challenge, so there are three possible responses:

(a)   to say that the apparently paradoxical conclusion is, after all, acceptable;

(b)   to deny E1; or

(c)   to deny G1.

Hempel himself makes the first of these responses. One could argue for it as follows. First, we must bear in mind that "confirm" is

---

5   The proof of equivalence may seem incomplete: The definition of equivalence also required that if R2 is true, so is R1, and if R2 is false, so is R1; yet these issues were not explicitly addressed. However, classical logic has it that, for any propositions P and Q, the truth of

If P is false, then Q is false

ensures the truth of

if Q is true, then P is true.

Likewise classical logic has it that the truth of

If P is true, then Q is true

ensures the truth of

If Q is false, then P is false.

Given these implications of classical logic, what is said in the text *does* establish the equivalence of R1 and R2.

being used in a technical way. It does not follow from the supposition that a white shoe *confirms* that all ravens are black that observing a white shoe puts you in a position reasonably to believe that all ravens are black. Second, there are cases in which it seems quite natural, or at least much less absurd, to allow that P1 confirms that all ravens are black – that is, that P1 could make a positive contribution to some good evidence for the hypothesis. Suppose that we are on an ornithological field trip. We have seen several black ravens in the trees and formulate the hypothesis that all ravens are black. We then catch sight of something white in a topmost branch. For a moment we tremble for the hypothesis, fearing a counterinstance – fearing, that is, that we have found a white raven. A closer look reveals that it is a shoe. In this situation, we are more likely to agree that a white shoe confirms the hypothesis. Hempel tells a similar story for a more realistic case. Investigating the hypothesis that all sodium salts burn yellow, we come across something that does not burn yellow. When we discover that the object is a lump of ice, we regard the experiment as having confirmed the hypothesis.

The first point appeals to the idea that some complicated story must be told in order to link confirmation to having good reason to believe. Furthermore, in the telling, it will be apparent why observing white shoes, despite their confirmatory character with respect to the hypothesis that all ravens are black, does not normally contribute to giving one good reason to believe the hypothesis. We cannot assess the suggestion until we know the details of this story.

The second of these points emphasizes that confirmation, as we normally think of it, is not an absolute notion but is relative to what background information we possess. Making this point leaves unstarted the task of specifying how the technical notion of confirmation – which, so far, has been taken as absolute – should be modified so as to take account of this relativity.

Perhaps these points can be developed so as to justify the first response, (a); but I shall now turn to the other possible responses.

Response (b) is to deny E1. For example, one might simply insist that anything that confirms a generalization must be an instance of it. This avoids the paradox and is inconsistent with E1, but it is very hard to justify. For example, suppose that we are investigating an outbreak of Legionnaires' disease. Our hypothesis is that the source of the infection was the water at St George's school, consumed by all the children who attended last week. Will only an instance of the generalization "All pupils attending St. George's last week contracted Legionnaires' disease" confirm it? Imagine that we find some St. George's children who are free from the disease, but that it then turns out they they missed school last week. We would normally count this as evidence in favor of our hypothesis – some potential and highly relevant counterinstances have been eliminated – and yet these children are not instances of the hypothesis.

There is a more general argument against the rejection of E1. Suppose we find some data that confirm two hypotheses, H1 and H2. It is standard practice to reason as follows: H3 is a consequence of H1 and H2, so to the extent that H1 and H2 are confirmed, so is H3. For example, if we had data that confirmed both the hypothesis that all anorexics are zinc-deficient and the hypothesis that everyone who is zinc-deficient is zinc-intolerant, the data would surely confirm the hypothesis that all anorexics are zinc-intolerant. However, if we allow that data confirm the *a priori* knowable consequences of hypotheses they confirm, we have in effect allowed E1.[6]

The third possible response to the paradox is to reject G1. This is both the most popular response, and also, I believe, the correct one. The Paradox of the Ravens already gives us some reason to reject it, if the other responses are unsatisfactory. The paradox of "grue," to be considered in the next section, gives a decisive reason for rejecting it. Moreover, there are quite straightforward counterexamples to it. Consider, for example, the hypothesis that all snakes inhabit regions other than Ireland. According to G1, a snake found outside Ireland confirms the hypothesis; but however we pile up the instances, we get no evidence for the hypothesis. Quite the contrary: The more widespread we find the distribution of snakes to be, the more unlikely it becomes that Ireland is snakefree. A non-Irish snake does not confirm the hypothesis, since it makes no positive contribution to the evidence in favor of the hypothesis, and may even count against it.

Rejecting G1 resolves the paradox, but it leaves us in a rather unsatisfactory position regarding confirmation: We have made very little progress toward uncovering the principles that underlie our discrimination between good and bad evidence. The next paradox brings to light more difficulties in the path of this project.

---

6   Q: How does this follow?

4.1.3. "Grue"

According to G1, green emeralds confirm the hypothesis that all emeralds are green. Now consider the predicate "grue," invented by Nelson Goodman [1955] with an eye to showing the inadequacy of G1. The meaning of "grue" ensures, by stipulation, that a thing x counts as *grue* if and only if it meets either of the following conditions:

Gr1. x is green and has been examined, or
Gr2. x is blue and has not been examined.[7]

The class of grue things is thus, by definition, made up of just the examined green things together with the unexamined blue things. All examined emeralds, being all of them green, count as grue, by Gr1. It follows from G1 that the hypothesis that all emeralds are grue is confirmed by our data: Every emerald we have examined is a confirming instance because it was green. This is absurd. If the hypothesis that all emeralds are grue is true, then unexamined emeralds (supposing that there are any) are blue. This we all believe is false, and certainly not confirmed by our data. G1 must be rejected.[8]

What is paradoxical is that a seeming truth, G1, leads, by apparently correct reasoning, to a seeming falsehood: that our data concerning emeralds confirm the hypothesis that they are all grue.[9] The paradox relates to the problem of *characterization* – of saying what kinds of

---

[7]   There has been controversy about how Goodman defines "grue." He writes that "grue" is to be introduced so that:

it applies to all things examined before t just in case they are green but to other things just in case they are blue. ([1955, p. 74)

The time t is arbitrary, and was introduced on Goodman's previous page. In giving my account, I have imagined ourselves being at that time. For discussion of some alternative interpretations, see Jackson [1975].

[8]   Goodman [1955], p. 74:

although we are well aware which of the two incompatible predictions [sc., "All emeralds subsequently examined will be green," "All emeralds subsequently examined will be grue"] is genuinely confirmed, they are equally well confirmed according to our definition [of confirmation – a definition close to G1].

[9]   Q*: An alternative presentation of the paradox identifies the apparently unacceptable conclusion as being that the same body of data can confirm the *inconsistent* hypotheses that all emeralds are green and that all emeralds are grue. Is it unthinkable that a body of data should confirm inconsistent hypotheses?

evidence we take to be good, or what sorts of inductive argument we take to be legitimate – because we need to say what makes us treat green and grue differently. G1 does not discriminate the cases.

Notice that the conclusion is unacceptable even if we recall that "confirms" is being used in a technical sense: It is not equivalent to "gives us good reason to believe," but means only something like "would make a positive contribution to a good reason for believing." It strikes us as unacceptable to suppose that an examined green emerald makes any contribution at all to giving a good reason for supposing that all emeralds are grue.[10]

We have already seen in connection with the ravens (section 4.1.2) that there is a case for rejecting G1; that case is, of course, strengthened by the present Grue Paradox. If we reject G1, then the paradox is, for the moment, resolved, for we shall have said that an apparently acceptable premise is not really acceptable. However, what can we put in its place? It would seem that something like G1 must be true. Is there an appropriate modification? If not, then the Grue Paradox remains unresolved; for to say that there is no appropriate modification of G1 is to say that there are no principles governing what makes a body of data confirm a hypothesis. This seems as unacceptable as the view that green emeralds confirm the hypothesis that all emeralds are grue.

Several suggestions have been made. Most of them can be seen as falling into one of two patterns:

1. The blame is placed on the word "grue," which is said to be of a particularly nasty kind, rather than on the structure of G1. All we need is a general principle for excluding the *grue*some words, and G1 will be acceptable for the remainder.

2. The blame is placed not so much on "grue" as on the attempt to formulate a principle, like G1, that takes no account at all of *background information* – information that is always in play in any real-life case of evidence or confirmation.

---

[10] We could rework the paradox using "gives good reason to believe" rather than "confirms." Our observations of emeralds, we suppose, give us good reason to believe that all emeralds are green. "Parity of reasoning" seems to require that our observations of emeralds also give us good reason to believe that they are all grue. If we tried to identify what this parity of reasoning consisted in, we would no doubt finger G1 or some very similar principle.

If we try the first response, the difficulty is to say exactly what is nasty about "grue." It is not enough to say that "grue" is an invented word, rather than one that occurs naturally in our language. Scientists often have to invent words (like "electron") or use old words in new ways (like "mass"), but it would be extravagant to infer that these new or newly used words cannot figure in confirmable generalizations.

It is more appealing to say that what is wrong with "grue" is that it implicitly mentions a specific time in its definition. Its definition appeals to what has *already* been examined, and this refers to the time at which the definition is made. In this respect, "grue" and "green" differ sharply, for there is no *verbal* definition of "green" at all, and so it is not the case that the definition of "green" involves reference to a particular time.

However, if we were to restrict G1 to generalizations in which there is no reference to a time, we would make it too restrictive. For example, the generalization "In Tudor times, most agricultural innovations were made in the north of the country" is one that could be confirmed or disconfirmed on the pattern of G1. In addition, G1 would not be restrictive enough. The structure of the Grue Paradox is preserved if we can find a way of picking out just the emeralds we have already examined. We might do this by giving each one a name, e_1, e_2, ...; or it might be that all and only the emeralds so far examined have come from a certain emerald mine (now exhausted); or something of the kind. Then we could define a predicate equivalent to "grue" without mentioning a time: In the one case we could say that it is to apply to any of e_1, e_2, ... just on condition that that thing is green, and to anything else just in case it is blue; in the other case we could say that it is to apply to everything taken from a certain mine just on condition that it is green, and to anything else just on condition that it is blue. Therefore it is not of the essence of the paradox that the definition of "grue" mentions a time.

There are other ways of trying to say what is nasty about "grue." Goodman's own attempt has at least superficial similarities to one I rejected earlier. He says that what is wrong with "grue" is that it is not "well-entrenched"; that is, the class of entities to which it applies is a class that has not been alluded to much – indeed, at all – in the making of predictions. To treat being poorly entrenched as sufficient for being incapable of figuring in confirmable generalizations seems to put an intolerable block on scientific innovativeness. Though Goodman is well aware of this problem, there is room for doubt about whether he deals with it successfully.[11]

I now want to consider a response of the other kind I mentioned: not restricting G1 by limiting it to generalizations that do not contain words sharing the supposed nasty features of "grue," whatever these features may be; but rather restricting G1 by appeal to background information. Intuitively, what is wrong with supposing that our information about examined emeralds gives us any reason for thinking that all emeralds are grue is that we know that the examined ones are grue only in virtue of having been examined. We do not believe that our examining the emeralds had any "real" effect on them. We believe that if they had not been examined they would not have been grue. What makes it so absurd to suppose, on the basis of our data, that all emeralds are grue is that we know that the unexamined ones lack the property in virtue of which the examined ones *are* grue: namely, having been examined. An initial attempt to formulate this thought might look like this:

> **G2.** A hypothesis "All F's are G's" is confirmed by its instances if and only if there is no property H such that the F's in the data are H, and if they had not been H, they would not have been G.[12]

We might try to support G2 by applying this to the following case, which in some respects looks similar to the grue emeralds. Suppose that we are gathering evidence about the color of lobsters, but unfortunately we have access only to boiled ones. All the lobsters in our sample are pink. Moreover, we know that the lobsters in the sample are pink only in virtue of having been boiled. Then it would be absurd for us to think that our sample confirms the hypothesis that all lobsters are pink. Here the hypothesis is "All lobsters (F) are pink (G)," and H

---

[11] For his discussion of the problem, see Goodman [1955], esp. p. 97ff. Goodman's theory of entrenchment is more sophisticated than my very brief mention of it would suggest.

[12] Cf. Jackson [1975]. It is no doubt true that Goodman's overall project would preclude him from accepting this version of G2 because it contains a subjunctive conditional ("If it had not been that ..., it would not have been that ..."). However, the current project is simply to address what I have called the problem of characterization (section 4.1.1), and it is unclear that any prohibition upon the use of subjunctive conditionals attends this project.

is the property of having been boiled. Because the lobsters in the sample are boiled, and had they not been boiled would not have been pink, the data do not meet the condition imposed by G2 for confirming the hypothesis.

The lobster case brings to light a difficulty, or series of difficulties, connected with G2. We start to uncover them if we ask: How do we know that the lobsters in the sample would not have been pink had they not been boiled? It would seem that if we know this, then we know that some lobsters are not pink at all times, and thus we are in a position to know that the hypothesis is false.

This shows that we can explain, without appealing to G2, why the evidence for the hypothesis that all lobsters are pink was deficient. A body of evidence fails to confirm any hypothesis to which it contains a counterinstance. However, the case in addition brings to light something more fundamental: that G2, as it stands, does not require our *body of data* to contain the proposition that there is no *H* such that the examined *F*'s would not have been *G* had they not been *H*. It requires only that this proposition be true. What would be relevant to G2 would thus be a variant of the lobster case in which all observed lobsters are pink, but we, the observers, do not realize that they are pink only because they have been boiled. G2 does *not rule* that, in this state of ignorance, our data confirm the generalization that all lobsters are pink.[13] Is this acceptable?

This raises an important issue. If it sounds wrong to say that the person who has observed only pink lobsters, and who knows nothing of the connection between boiling and color (and perhaps does not even know that the sample lobsters have been boiled), lacks data that would confirm the hypothesis that all lobsters are pink, this is because we intuitively feel that evidence should be *transparent*. By this I mean that we intuitively feel that if a body of data is evidence for a hypothesis, then we ought to be able to tell that this is so merely by examining the data and the hypothesis: One ought, in other words, to be able to tell that this is so *a priori*. This intuitive feeling might be supported by the following argument. Suppose that no evidence is, in this sense, transparent. Then, a claim to the effect that a body of data *D* confirms a hypothesis *H* will itself be a hypothesis needing confirmation. We shall need to cast around for data to confirm, or disconfirm, the

---

[13] Q: How would G2 need to be modified for it to rule that, in this variant lobster case, our data do *not confirm* the generalization?

hypothesis that *D* confirms *H*. It looks as if we are set on an infinite regress, and that we could never have any reason to suppose that anything confirms anything unless evidence is transparent.

Not all evidence is transparent. Spots can confirm the hypothesis that the patient has measles, but one needs medical knowledge to recognize that the data, the spots, are thus related to the hypothesis: One needs to know that only people, or most people, with spots of this kind have measles. In other words, it is clear that in many cases the evidence is not transparent. In any case, the most the argument of the preceding paragraph could show is that *some* evidence needs to be transparent, since this is all that is needed to block the alleged regress.

If we feel that some evidence should be transparent, we shall surely feel that an example is the limiting case in which everything that *can* be included among the data *has* beeen included. In this case, we shall feel that one ought to be able to tell *a priori*, without further investigation, which hypotheses these data confirm. However, this is not guaranteed by G2, for two reasons.

First, for some hypotheses, "All *F*'s are *G*'s," our data may include plenty of instances and no counterinstances but fail to contain either the proposition "There is no *H* such that all examined *F*'s are *H* and would not have been *G* had they not been *H*" or its negation. In this case, if G2 is true, we could not tell *a priori* whether our data confirm the hypothesis, since we could not tell whether the condition it places on the instances of the hypothesis obtains or not.

Second, it is a debatable question whether this condition *could* properly be included among our data. One might hold that all data must, in the end, be observations, and that a condition such as "There is no *H* such that all examined *F*'s are *H* and would not have been *G* had they not been *H*" is not something immediately available to observation, and so cannot be a datum.

These objections point in controversial directions. The second objection presupposes a form of *foundationalism,* which is highly controversial. Perhaps, contrary to the presupposition, there is nothing in the intrinsic nature of a proposition that qualifies it as a datum; thus, on occasion, the counterfactual condition could count as a datum. If this is allowed, then we could envisage a variant of G2 that meets the first of the two objections.

> **G3.** A hypothesis "All *F*'s are *G*'s" is confirmed by a body of data containing its instances if and only if the data also contain the

proposition "There is no such property H such that the F's in the data are H, and if they had not been H, they would not have been G."

Like G2, this does not rule that "All emeralds are grue" is confirmed by its instances, if we can allow that our data contain the proposition "There is a property, namely *being examined,* such that the emeralds in the data have been examined, and had they not been examined, they would not have been grue." It has the further merit of being consistent with transparency: Whether or not a body of data confirms a hypothesis depends only on the body and the hypothesis themselves, and not on other, perhaps inaccessible, facts. However, it has the apparently dubious feature that smaller bodies of data can confirm more than can larger bodies.

To see how this works, imagine two people, both confronted with pink boiled lobsters, and both concerned to consider the question of whether their data confirm "All lobsters are pink." One person does not realize that all the lobsters he has seen have been boiled, or else does not realize that boiling them affects their color. If G3 is correct, that person's data do confirm the hypothesis "All lobsters are pink." The other person, by contrast, knows that the lobsters would not have been pink had they not been boiled. G3 does not entail that that person's data confirm the hypothesis that all lobsters are pink. If you know more, your data may confirm less.

This feature is one that should come as no surprise. A body of data full of instances of a generalization, and containing no counter-instances, may confirm the generalization, though the same body enriched by a counterinstance would not. Still, G3 needs refinement. For one thing, it still leads, in conjunction with E1, to the Ravens Paradox.[14] For another thing, we need to relax it a little, as the following example shows.

Suppose you find, year after year, that although all the other vegetables in your garden are attacked by pests, your leeks are always pest-free. Would it be reasonable to conclude that leeks are immune to pests? Let us suppose that you know no proposition to the effect that your leeks would not have been healthy had they not possessed some property P. According to G3, the hypothesis that all leeks are immune

---

[14]   Q: How can one "prove" the Ravens Paradox using G3 rather than G1?

to pests is confirmed by your data; but I think that we should not, in fact, put much confidence in the hypothesis, given the data. Even if one knows no proposition of the relevant kind, one may strongly suspect that *there is* one, even though one does not know it. One knows in a general way that susceptibility to pests is likely to be affected by such factors as the nature of the soil, how strongly the plant grows, and what other vegetation is around. Even though your data do not include a proposition that selects a factor that explains the pest-free quality of your leeks, you might well believe that *there is* a proposition of this kind. If so, you should not put much faith in the hypothesis that all leeks, including those grown in very different conditions, are immune to pests.

If it is to deliver the results we want in such cases, the proviso in G3 must be understood in such a way that:

(a) The data must not contain even the proposition that *there is* a proposition to the effect that the F's are G only in virtue of being H; and

(b) The background information in general, and this in particular, do not have to be *known* or be *certain*.

All other things being equal, the fact that we think it quite *likely* that there are conditions under which leeks suffer from pests is enough to diminish, or even perhaps cancel, the confirmatory impact of our pest-free leeks. I shall assume that these modifications to G3 have been made.

G3 entails that the hypothesis that all emeralds are grue *is* confirmed by the data consisting just of propositions of the form "This is an emerald," "This has been examined," and so on; but it does not entail that this hypothesis is confirmed by the body of data, including background information, that we in fact possess. That body of data includes the proposition that the examined emeralds would not have been grue had they not been examined; that is, it includes a proposition of the form "There is a property H (*having been examined*) such that the emeralds would not have been grue had they not had H."

Does G3 rule out enough? One might in particular have doubts about whether it should allow that the grue hypothesis is confirmed by the narrower body of data. These doubts might be to some extent assuaged by reflecting that a body of data can confirm a hypothesis that they do not make it rational to believe. We could insist that instances confirm, in the sense of making a positive contribution to good grounds for belief, while not on their own constituting such grounds.

The following example is designed to put this view to the test. We have to try to imagine a case in which we have just the instances of a generalization, and absolutely no relevant background information at all. Suppose you come across a very large sack of marbles. You cannot see into the sack, but you manage to take out one marble at a time. You do this for a while, and all those you take out are green. By G3, the hypothesis that all the marbles are green, including the unseen ones still in the sack, is confirmed. However, I claim that you still do not have good reason to believe that all the marbles in the sack are green. Remember that you are not allowed to bring to bear any background information in the form of suppositions about how the marbles came to be in the sack. The hypothesis that they were put there by a collector of marbles must be, for you, no more likely than that they were put there by a philosopher wanting to make a point about confirmation theory. Moreover, you can form no reasonable belief about whether you are, or are not, selecting the marbles "at random." Perhaps the only way to extract a marble is to press a lever at the side of the sack. You have no idea whether they are being dealt from the top or in some other order, or whether the mechanism selects them in some genuinely indeterministic fashion. Under these circumstances, it seems to me quite doubtful whether our run of green marbles gives us good grounds for believing that all the marbles in the sack are green. In particular, there does not seem to be much difference in the justification of the view that they are all green and the view that they are all grue. It must be stressed that such situations are bound to be rare. Perhaps we have to imagine ourselves on an alien planet, governed by unknown physical laws, to ensure that we are really not bringing background information to bear, as we normally would.

We perhaps incline to think that if *all* we knew about emeralds consisted in a large number of green samples, it is not merely that the hypothesis that all emeralds are green would be confirmed by our data: In addition, we would be justified in believing it. This, I think, is an illusion. In forming this view, I think we unconsciously bring to bear background information concerning the color constancy of most gemstones, together with the supposition that emeralds fall into this general category. Take this supposition away, and there can be no move from confirmation to justified belief. One can see this by comparing the case in which all the tomatoes I have ever come across are green. This would give me good reason to believe that all tomatoes are green only if I had good reason to think that the sample tomatoes were somehow typical; but of course I can have no such reason.

I claim that G3 will remove anything puzzling about the Grue Paradox. It explains how, as things are, our data do not confirm that all emeralds are grue; and although it concedes that other, narrower bodies of data might confirm this generalization, it would be reasonable to make the further claim that, in this case, confirmation falls short of good grounds for belief. However, as should be obvious from the rest of the discussion, this leaves a great deal to be said about the nature of confirmation and its ultimate connection with the notion of rational belief.

The Grue Paradox has been held to have more distant ramifications. To gesture toward these, let us consider a corollary that Goodman stresses:

> Regularities are where you find them, and you can find them anywhere.

The old idea – found, for example, in Hume – was that the reasoning from experience that we take to be legitimate is that in which we extrapolate regularities obtaining within our experience to portions of the world that lie outside our experience. One thing that Goodman's "grue" shows is that this is, at best, a highly incomplete account. The question is: What is to count as a regularity? The regular connection between being an emerald and being green? *And* the regular connection between being an emerald and being grue? Our original problem reemerges in this form: Either we can give no account of what a regularity is, in which case the account that uses the notion is useless; or else we give an account of regularity that includes the undesirable emerald–grue regularity as well as the desirable emerald–green one.

This relatively narrow point about confirmation suggests a deeper metaphysical one: that whether a series of events counts as a regularity depends upon how we choose to describe it. This has suggested to some a quite thoroughgoing conventionalism, according to which there is no separating how the world is in itself from the conventions we bring to bear in describing and classifying it. To others, it has had the effect of deepening their skepticism about the legitimacy of inductive reasoning. If there are endless regularities that we could have extrapolated, what makes it rational to pick on the ones we in fact do? It is bad enough having to justify extrapolating a regularity, but it is worse when one must, in addition, justify selecting one rather than any of the countless other regularities in the data to extrapolate. To yet others, the Grue Paradox has suggested that there is something quite undetermined, at least at the individual level, about our concepts. Wittgenstein asked us to consider someone who, having added 2 to numbers all the way up to 1,000, continues this way − 1,004, 1,008, ... − and yet protests that he is "going on in the same way." We could define a gruelike operator "+*" as follows: $x +* 2 = x + 2$, if $x < 1,000$; otherwise $x +* 2 = x + 4$. It has been suggested that there are no facts, or at least no individual facts, that make it true of us that we use concepts like *green* and + rather than concepts like *grue* and +*.

The impact of grue thus goes well beyond the problems of finding a nonparadoxical account of our notion of confirmation.

4.2.   THE UNEXPECTED EXAMINATION

The teacher tells the class that sometime during the next week she will give an examination. She will not say on which day for, she says, she wants it to be a surprise. On the face of it, there is no reason why the teacher, despite having made this announcement, should not be able to do exactly what she has announced: give the class an unexpected examination. It will not be totally unexpected, since the class will know, or at least have good reason to believe, that it will occur sometime during the next week. However, surely it could be unexpected in this sense: that on the morning of the day on which it is given, the class will have no good reason to believe that it will occur on *that* day, even though they knew, or had good reason to believe, the teacher's announcement. Cannot the teacher achieve this aim by, say, giving the examination on Wednesday?

The class reasons as follows. Let us suppose that the teacher will carry out her threat, in both its parts: That is, she will give an examination, and it will be unexpected. Then the teacher cannot give the examination on Friday (assuming this to be the last possible day of the week); for, by the time Friday morning arrives, and we know that all the previous days have been examination-free, we would have every reason to expect the examination to occur on Friday. So leaving the examination until Friday is inconsistent with giving an *unexpected* examination. For similar reasons, the examination cannot be held on

Thursday. Given our previous conclusion that it cannot be delayed until Friday, we would know, when Thursday morning came, and the previous days had been examination-free, that it would have to be held on Thursday. So if it were held on Thursday, it would not be unexpected. Thus it cannot be held on Thursday. Similar reasoning supposedly shows that there is no day of the week on which it can be held, and so supposedly shows that the supposition that the teacher can carry out her threat must be rejected. This is paradoxical, for it seems plain that the teacher *can* carry out her threat.

Something must be wrong with the way in which the class reasoned; but what?

The class's argument falls into two parts: One applies to whether there can be an unexpected examination on the last day, Friday; the other takes forward the negative conclusion on this issue, and purports to extend it to the other days.

Let us begin by looking more closely at the first part. On Friday morning, the possibilities can be divided up as follows:

(a)   The examination will take place on Friday and the class will expect this.

(b)   The examination will take place on Friday and the class will not expect this.

(c)   The examination will not take place on Friday and the class will expect this.

(d)   The examination will not take place on Friday and the class will not expect this.

When we speak of the class's expectations, we mean their rational or well-grounded ones. It is not to the point that they may have expectations to which they are not entitled, or lack expectations to which they are entitled. For example, it is not to the point that the class might irrationally (without entitlement or justification) believe that the examination would take on Wednesday. Even it it then did take place on Wednesday, this would not show that the teacher's announcement was false, for she said that the class would have *no good reason* to believe it would occur when it did.

The overall structure of the class's argument is meant to be a *reductio ad absurdum:* They take as a supposition that the teacher's announcement is true, then aim to show that this leads to a contradiction, and hence that the supposition must be rejected. In this first part of the argument, the supposition is used to show that that the examination cannot occur on Friday. This is extended to every day of the week in the second part of the argument, so that, in the end, the supposition is rejected. Thus the teacher's announcement is disproved.

Given that the examination has not occurred on the previous days, at most possibility (b) is consistent with the truth of the teacher's announcement. The class's argument aims to show that (b) is not a real possibility.

The idea is that the class can infer that if the examination occurs on Friday, then the announcement is false, contrary to the supposition. The inference is based on the consideration that the class will know that Friday is the last possible day for the examination. So, given the supposition that the teacher's announcement is true, they would expect the examination, were it to occur on Friday; but this is inconsistent with the truth of the announcement. If we hold on to the supposition, the examination cannot take place on Friday.

That this argument is not straightforward can be brought out by the following. Imagine yourself in the class, and it is Friday morning. There is surely a real question, which you may well feel that you do not know how to answer: Has the teacher forgotten or changed her mind, or will the examination indeed take place that day? It would seem that this doubt is enough to ensure that if it does take place that day, it will be unexpected: The class was not entitled to expect it.

The class's argument is meant to circumvent this difficulty by using the truth of the teacher's announcement as a supposition – one that, in the end, is going to be rejected. Given this supposition, the class on Friday morning can rule out the nonoccurrence of the examination. On the other hand, it can also rule out its occurrence – and this is what is meant to show that, if the supposition is true, the examination cannot occur on Friday.

However, it is a mistake to think that the supposition merely of the *truth* of the teacher's announcement will do the required work. To see this, imagine ourselves once more among the class on Friday morning. Suppose that the teacher's announcement is true but that we do not know or even believe this. Then we may not believe that the examination will occur. This is enough to make the truth of the announcement possible: If the examination does occur, we shall not have expected it. This shows a fallacy in the reasoning as so far presented. Merely supposing, for *reductio,* that the teacher's announcement is true is not enough to establish that the examination will not be held on Friday. At that point in the argument, we need as a supposition that we *know* that the teacher's announcement is true.[15]

If we are to have a paradoxical argument worth discussing, we need to make some changes. There are various ways in which one could do this; I shall consider two. The details are quite complicated: To make the discussion manageable, we shall soon need to use some abbreviations.

One modification we could make is to leave the announcement unchanged but alter the structure of the argument. Instead of taking the announcement itself as our supposition, we shall suppose that the class *knows* the truth of the announcement. This supposition is refutable, on Friday, by the considerations outlined. If on Friday we know that the announcement is true, we know that the examination will occur on Friday. If we know that the examination will occur on Friday, the announcement is not true. If the announcement is not true, then we do not know that it is true. The supposition that we know that it is true entails its own falsehood, and so can be rejected. Applying similar reasoning to the other days of the week, the upshot would be that the class can show that it cannot *know* that the annnouncement is true. This may seem paradoxical: Intuitively, we want to say that we knew, from the announcement, that there would be an examination sometime, though we did not know when, and so it was unexpected.

An alternative modification involves changing the announcement to include the fact that the class will not know, on the basis of the announcement, that the examination will take place on the day that it does. In a way that can only be made clear by some abbreviations, this will give us a valid argument for the conclusion that the announcement is false. If this is paradoxical, it is because it seems intuitively obvious that such an announcement could be true.

Let us call the original version of the argument OV, the first proposed modified version MV1, and the second proposed modified version MV2. Since the number of days of the week is irrelevant, let us simplify by supposing that there are just two possible examination days, Monday or Tuesday. For OV and MV1, I shall abbreviate the announcement as:

---

[15]   This point is made by Quine [1953].

A1. I shall give you an examination on either Monday or Tuesday, and you will not know – or have good reason to believe – on the morning of the examination that it will occur that day.

The other abbreviations are as follows:

M for "the examination occurs on Monday";
T for "the examination occurs on Tuesday";.
$K_M(...)$ for "the class knows on Monday morning that ...";
    and
$K_T(...)$ for "the class knows on Tuesday morning that ...."[16]

We can express A1 symbolically as:

([M and not-K_M(M)] or [T and not-K_T(T)]) and not both M
    and T.

(That is, either there will be an examination on Monday and the class does not know this on Monday morning, or there will be an examination on Tuesday and the class does not know this on Tuesday morning; and there will be an examination on at most one morning.)[17]

OV can be represented as follows:

1. Suppose A1.
2.   Suppose not-M
3. K_T(not-M)   [from 2 + memory]
4.   If not-M, T.   [by the definition of A1]
5. K_T(T)   [from 3 + 4]
6.   If K_T(T) and not-M,
            then not-A1   [by the definition of A1]

---

[16] I offer no view about whether believing or knowing are to be properly represented by an operator or by a predicate. Those who prefer the operator treatment will have to read "A1," as it occurs in the formal argument, as short for "A1 is true." Those who prefer the predicate treatment will have to read various expressions within the scope of K as names of (equiform) expressions, rather than as expressions in use. It may be worth reminding those familiar with these matters that Montague and Kaplan [1960] present the paradox using the predicate treatment to avert the suspicion that operators are to blame (see p. 272). Asher and Kamp [1986] take the Knower Paradox (discussed later in this section) to bear essentially on the question of what is the appropriate account of propositional attitude constructions.

[17] **Q:** Would it be better to have A1 abbreviate the following?
(M or T) and not-K_M(M) and not-K_T(T)

7.	not-A1	[from 2, 5, + 6]
8.	So, still supposing A1, we must conclude that M (and so not-T)	
9.	$K_M(M)$	[from 8 + A1]
10.	If $K_M(M)$ and not-T, then not-A1	[definition of A1]
11.	not-A1	[from 8, 9, + 10]
12.	not-A1	[from 1 + 11]

The overall shape of the argument is *reductio ad absurdum:* One makes an assumption in order to show that it leads to a contradiction and so must be rejected. In the present case, the supposition of A1 is supposed to lead eventually to the conclusion that A1 is false. (Indentation is used to show that – and how – some steps of the argument occur within the scope of a supposition.)[18] It seems that we intuitively hold that A1 can be true; and that clash constitutes the paradox.

OV suffers from the defect that no adequate justification is provided for step (5). The idea is meant to be this: If A1 is true, then the examination must occur on Tuesday if it does not occur on Monday; so if we knew the examination did not occur on Monday, we would know that it would occur on Tuesday. However, this is not a sound inference: We would also need to *know* that the examination must occur on Tuesday if it does not occur on Monday.[19]

---

[18] I hope that the intended structure of the argument will be self-explanatory, but some observations may be useful for those unused to seeing arguments presented in this sort of way.

What is the difference between lines (7), (11), and (12)? Each has the same conclusion, but it has been reached from different suppositions. At (7), as the extra indent shows, the argument claims that we have reached *not-A1* on the basis of supposing that A1 is true and that not-M is true. This would mean that we have reached a contradiction: Since anything entails itself, the supposition of both A1 and not-M leads to the contradiction that A1 and not-A1. We must therefore reject at least one of these. Line (8) claims that if we hold on to A1, we must reject not-M (equivalently, T). At line (11), *not-A1* depends only on the supposition of A1 itself. In other words, at this point we have shown that A1 entails to its own negation. This is enough to show that, on the basis of *no* suppositions at all, we can infer the falsehood of A1, since anything entailing its own negation is false, and this is what (12), by having *no* indent, expresses.

[19] Q: Does this criticism also apply to (9)?

MV1 can be represented as follows:

1. Suppose K(A1)
    2. Suppose not-M
        3. K_T(not-M)   [from 2 and memory]
        4. If not-M, T   [by the definition of A1]
        5. K_T(If not-M, T)   [by supposition 1]
        6. K_TT   [from 3 + 5]
        7. If K_TT, then not-A1   [definition of A1]
        8. If not-A1, then not-K(A1)   [only the truth is known]
        9. If K_TT then not-K(A1)   [from 7 + 8]
    10. So, given K(A1), we must
        conclude that M (and so not-T)
    11. K_M(M)   [from 10][20]
    12. If K_M(M) and M, then not-A1   [definition of A1]
    13. not-A1   [from 10, 11, + 12]
    14. If not-A1, then not-K(A1)   [only the truth is known]
    15. not-K(A1)   [from 13 + 14]
16. not-K(A1)   [from 1 + 15]

Even if MV1 is valid (and footnote 20 gives a reason for doubt on this point), it is questionable whether there is anything paradoxical in this conclusion. To have a paradox, we would need also to have an argument for the conclusion that K(A1). Perhaps it is just intuitively obvious that K(A1), given, if you like, the class's knowledge of the teacher's unimpeachable reputation for veracity and constancy of purpose; but suppose someone failed to share this intuition?

---

[20] The argument is suspect at this point. We have supposedly proved M [at (10)] on the basis of K(A1). It is quite plausible to hold that this means that we can know the corresponding conditional, viz.:

If K(A1), then M.

However, to obtain K_MM from K[If K(A1), then M] would appear to require as a premise not merely K(A1), but K[K(A1)]. We should avoid obtaining the latter by the dubious schema:

If K(φ), then K[K(φ)].

However, it could be argued that, in the envisaged case, K(A1) would ensure K[K(A1)]: Nothing relevant to whether the class knows A1 would be unknown to it.

Q: Why is this last principle – if K(φ), then K[K(φ)] – dubious?

If not-K(A1), then it is very easy for A1 to be true: The class will not on the basis of A1 have any expectations, since the students can establish that they cannot know A1. This gives the teacher plenty of scope for surprising them.

However, the class can also go through the reasoning of the preceding paragraph: "Our proof that A1 cannot be known shows us how easy it is for A1 to be true. If it *can* be true, then, given the teacher's proven veracity and determination, we have every reason to believe that it *is* true." If the class is led by this consideration to believe the announcement, then there is a case for thinking that their belief amounts to knowledge. So it seems that *if* the argument is valid, we have a paradox.[21]

MV2 requires a different announcement:

A2. Either [M and not-K_M(If A2, then M)] or [T and not-K_T (If A2, then T)].

(That is, the examination will take place on Monday or Tuesday, but you will not know on the basis of this announcement which day it will be.) Notice that A2 differs from A1 in a striking respect: The specification of A2 refers to A2 itself; in other words, A2 is a *self-referential* announcement.

MV2 can be represented as follows:

1. Suppose A2
   2. Suppose not-M
      3. K_T(not-M)   [from (2) + memory]

---

[21] Once one starts thinking about knowledge, one can rather easily convince oneself that there is less of it than one might have thought. So I would not be surprised if someone were to say, "We could not *know* that the teacher would carry out her threat, however reliable we knew her to have been in the past. The most we would be entitled to is the justified belief that she would."

Q: Rework MV1 in terms of justified belief rather than knowledge. (You will probably find you have to make an inference from "It was rational for the class to believe the teacher's announcement when it was made" to "It would be rational for the class to believe the teacher's announcement on the morning of the last day, if the exam had not yet been given." Is this inference sound? Is the parallel inference in the case of knowledge sound? At what points was it assumed in the arguments displayed above?)

    4. K_T(If not-M, then if A2,
        then T)   [the class understands A2]
    5. K_T(If A2, then T)   [from 3 + 4]
    6. not-A2   [from 2 + 5]
  7. M   [from 1, 2, + 6]
8. If A2, then M   [summarizing 1–7]
9. K_M(If A2, then M)   [the proved is known]
10. If K_M(If A2, then M), then if A2,
    then not-M   [from definition of A2]
11. If A2, then not-M   [from 9 + 10]
12. not-A2   [from 8 + 11]

MV2 purports to prove that A2 is not true. This is paradoxical only if we have some good reason to think that it is, or could be, true. We seem to have some reason: Have we not all been exposed to such threats of unexpected examinations? The form of A2 admittedly has the self-referential feature already noticed, but it is not clear that this should make any difference. When the teacher says that the examination is to be unexpected, what is clearly intended is that it be unexpected on any basis, including on the basis of this present announcement. So the intuitions that told us that A1 could be true, and could be known, should also tell us that A2 could be true. However, intuition may be less than wholly confident when faced with the validity of MV2.

Using a self-referential type of announcement, one can construct a further announcement, call it A3, that is certainly paradoxical. It has come to be called the Knower Paradox:[22]

A3. K(not-A3).

(That is, A3 is as follows: "The class knows that this very announcement is false.")

We can represent the argument that establishes both A3 and not-A3 as follows – call it **MV3**:

1. Suppose A3
    2. K(not-A3)   [definition of A3]
    3. not-A3   [what is known is true]
4. If A3, then not-A3   [summarizing 1–3]

---

[22] Cf. Montague and Kaplan [1960]. A similar paradox is in Buridan's Sophism 13; see Hughes [1982].

5. not-A3   [from 4]
6. not-K(not-A3)   [from 5 + definition of A3]
7. K(not-A3)   [5 + what is proved is known]

Lines (6) and (7) are contradictory.

In view of this result, we must examine carefully (a) the nature of the announcement and (b) the epistemic principles – the principles involving the nature of knowledge – used to reach the paradoxical conclusion. If there is anything wrong with the principles, then we may have to revise our views about the earlier arguments, for they, too, rest on these principles.

(a)   It is important to see that we cannot satisfy ourselves merely by saying that A3 is contradictory. A contradiction is false, whereas A3, if the argument MV3 is sound, is demonstrably true [see line (7)]. More hopeful would be to say that A3 is *unintelligible,* perhaps in part because of its self-referentiality. What, we might ask, does it *say*? What is it that it claims cannot be known? If we say it claims that it itself cannot be known, we seem to be grappling in thin air rather than genuinely answering the question.

Some of this doubt might be removed by changing the example. Suppose now that we have two teachers, X and Y. X says "What Y will say next is something you can know to be false." Y then says "What X has just said is true." It looks as though we have to count both utterances as intelligible, since in other contexts they certainly would have been intelligible, and even in this context we can understand X's without knowing what Y will say, and can understand Y's without knowing what X has said. However, in the context Y's announcement appears to be equivalent to A3. We could argue informally for the contradiction like this. Suppose Y is true (let X and Y now also abbreviate the respective teachers' remarks). Then X is true, so you can know Y to be false, so it is false. So the supposition that Y is true leads to the conclusion that it is false. Hence we can conclude that it is false [cf. MV3(5)]. Hence we can conclude that *we can know Y to be false.* However, if Y is false, then X is false; i.e., *we cannot know Y to be false.* So it seems we have an argument that has the essential features of A3, but that is not open to the charge that the announcement is unintelligible.[23]

---

[23]   Compare a similar line of argument in section 5.2, and in Burge [1978], p. 30.

(b)   Let us isolate the epistemic principles concerning knowledge appealed to in MV3. There are three: The first – call it EK1 – is what licenses the move from (2) to (3) in MV3. In its most general form it is that what is known is true. We could write it:

EK1.   If $K(\varphi)$, then φ.

The other point at which appeal to epistemic principles is made is the move at (7) from (5). It cannot be true that anything that is provable on the basis of no matter what assumptions is knowable. Given as assumption that $5 > 7$, I could perhaps prove that $5 > 6$, but obviously I could not *know* this. So the principle that we need at this point is that anything proved from known assumptions (or from no assumptions) is known.[24] We could write this as:

EK2.   If C is provable from $(P_1, ..., P_n)$ and $K(P_1, ..., P_n)$, then $K(C)$.

What assumptions (corresponding to P_1, etc.) are in play in the move from (5) to (7)? Just one: EK1. So, in order to apply EK2, we need to add:

EK3. $K(EK1)$.

Are these three principles plausible? Expressed informally they are the following:

EK1. What is known is true.
EK2. What is provable from things known is known.
EK3. It is known that what is known is true.

The first principle has sometimes been doubted on the grounds that, for example, people once knew that whales were fish; but this doubt is dispelled by the reflection that the correct account of the matter is that people *thought* they knew this, although they really did not. How could they have known it if it is not even true?

EK2 does not hold generally: We do not know all the infinitely many things that could be proved from what we know; we do not even believe all these things, if only because it would be beyond our powers

---

[24]   Compare with the principle sometimes called "epistemic closure":

If $K(\text{if } \varphi, \text{then } \psi)$ and $K(\varphi)$, then $K(\psi)$.

Q: Is EK2 is entailed by the closure principle? Does the converse entailment hold?

to bring them all to mind. However, this implausible aspect of EK2 is not required for the paradox, which only needs this much narrower claim: that at least one person who has constructed a correct proof of not-A3 from a known premise knows that not-A3.

The third principle cannot be seriously questioned, once we have granted the first. So the only doubt about the premises attaches to EK2. We could circumvent this by using an even weaker and very hard to controvert principle: What is provable from something known is *capable* of being known by a fully rational subject. With appropriate modifications to A3, we shall be able to prove a contradiction from principles that appear indubitable, together with the admission of the intelligibility of the teacher's announcement.[25]

It is very hard to know what to make of this paradox. One promising suggestion sees a similarity between it and the Liar Paradox (see section 5.2). Knowledge quite clearly involves the notion of truth, and the Liar Paradox shows that this notion can lead to paradox. So perhaps what is at fault in the concept of knowledge is the concept of truth it contains, as displayed in EK1; and perhaps the remedy consists in applying to knowledge whatever nonparadoxical elaboration of the notion of truth we can extract from consideration of the Liar Paradox.

The suggestion cannot be quite right for the following reason. Unlike knowledge, belief does not entail truth; yet a paradox rather like the Knower – we could call it the Believer – can be constructed in terms just of belief. Consider the following:

B$_1$. α does not believe what B$_1$ says.[26]

Question: Does α believe B$_1$ or not? If α does believe B$_1$, then he can see that he is believing something false. There is no gap between seeing that something is false and not believing it, so if α believes B$_1$, he does not believe it. Equally, however, if α does not believe B$_1$, then he can see that B$_1$ is true. There is no gap between seeing that something is true and believing it, so if α does not believe B$_1$ he believes it.

---

[25] Q: Provide the modified A3 (call it A4) and the appropriate argument, setting out the epistemic principles in detail.

[26] A version of the Believer analogous to the "What I am now saying is false" version of the Liar would be as follows:

The person now reading this sentence does not believe what it says.

The paradox depends on at least two assumptions:

1.   that α *can* see that, if he believes B_1, it is false, and if he does not believe it, it is true;
2.   that what α can see he *will* see.

Neither assumption would be capable of true generalization. For (1) to hold of α requires, among other things, that he be able to see that he is α. One could arguably envisage this not being true, if α had an unusually low level of self-awareness. For (2) to hold of α requires a positive level of intellectual energy: One does not always take advantage of one's epistemic opportunities. However, we have a paradox if we can make the following highly plausible assumption: that there is at least one person with the self-awareness and energy required to make (1) and (2) true of him (or her).

We can represent the argument to the contradiction, and the assumptions upon which it depends, in a manner analogous to the representation of the Knower Paradox.[27] We abbreviate "α believes that ( )" as "B( )"; then $B_1 = \text{not-}B(B_1)$.

1. Suppose $B(B_1)$
2. If $B(B_1)$, then $B[B(B_1)]$ [self-awareness]
    3. $B[B(B_1)]$ [from 1 + 2]
    4. $B[\text{If } B_1, \text{ then not-}B(B_1)]$ [α understands B_1]
    5. If $B[B(B_1)]$,
        then $\text{not-}B[\text{not-}B(B_1)]$ [rationality]
    6. $\text{not-}B[\text{not-}B(B_1)]$ [from 3 + 5]
    7. $\text{not-}B(B_1)$ [4, 6, + closure]
8. If $B(B_1)$, then $\text{not-}B(B_1)$ [summarizing 1–7]
9. $\text{not-}B(B_1)$ [from 8]
10. $B[\text{not-}B(B_1)]$ [from 9 + self-awareness]
11. $B(B_1)$ [from 10 + definition of B_1]

The unconditionally derived lines (9) and (11) are contradictory.

Let us examine the assumptions upon which the argument depends. The first principle to be used is what I have called "self-awareness." In its most general form it could be represented as follows:

EB1.   If $B(\varphi)$, then $B[B(\varphi)]$.

---

[27]   For a different version of the argument, see Burge [1978], esp. p. 29.

This is not very plausible. If it were true, then having one belief, say φ, would involve having infinitely many: that you believe that φ, that you believe you believe that φ, and so on. However, all that is required for the paradox are two instances of EB1: that if α believes B_1, under circumstances that can be as favorable as you like to self-awareness, then he will believe he does so; and if α does not believe B_1, then he will believe he does not. It seems impossible to deny that there could be a person of whom this is true.

The second assumption is that α understands B_1 and therefore realizes (and so believes), from the definition of B_1, that if B_1 then not-$B(B_1)$. Again, it seems impossible to deny that there could be a person who has this belief.

Next comes the principle called rationality. A generalization would be the following:

EB2.   If $B(\varphi)$ then not-$B(\text{not-}\varphi)$.

Put so generally, this is not plausible, since people in fact have contradictory beliefs without realizing it; but we need only impute a fairly modest degree of rationality to α in order for the premise needed at line (5) to obtain.

A generalization of the closure principle is this:

EB3.   If $B(\text{if } \varphi, \text{ then } \psi)$ and $B(\text{not-}\psi)$, then $B(\text{not-}\varphi)$.

For normal persons, this is not a plausible principle: We do not believe all the consequences of things we believe. However, it again seems easy to imagine that α verifies the particular case of the principle needed in the above argument.

Let us step back. A suggestion was that the Knower Paradox should be treated like the Liar Paradox, on the grounds that knowledge entails truth, and the Liar Paradox shows that the notion of truth requires special treatment. The point of introducing the Believer Paradox was to challenge this suggestion. Belief does not entail truth, yet belief gives rise to a paradox quite similar to the Knower.

The conclusion is that the reason given for treating the Knower and the Liar in similar ways is deficient. However, I shall suggest (in section 5.3) that there is another reason for thinking that the Knower, the Believer, and the Liar all call for a response of essentially the same kind.

BIBLIOGRAPHICAL NOTES

For Section 4.1.1

David Hume assumed that it was easy to answer the problem of characterization in the way envisaged in this section: The arguments we take to be legitimate are those in which it is assumed that the future will resemble the past. This suggestion is definitively refuted by the Grue Paradox. Hume [1738], Book I, Part III remains essential reading on the problem of the justification of induction, and on various connected issues, notably causation.

For Section 4.1.2

Hempel [1945] is a classic account of the Paradox of the Ravens and has generated a large literature. For a brief introduction to confirmation theory, see Schlesinger [1974a]. A useful collection of early papers is in Foster and Martin [1966].

For Section 4.1.3

The classic source of the Grue Paradox is Goodman [1955]. Like the Paradox of the Ravens, the Grue Paradox has generated a huge literature. My suggested modification of G1 derives from Jackson [1975], but the position is far from universally accepted.

The view that instances alone cannot make it reasonable to believe a generalization has been advocated by Foster [1983].

The example of "+*" comes from Kripke [1982]. Goodman's own philosophical development has been influenced by what he would regard as ramifications of the Grue Paradox – see Goodman [1978], p. 11.

For Section 4.2

A good early discussion is Quine [1953]. My main debt is to Montague and Kaplan [1960], and, for the Believer, to Burge [1978]. See "The Grid" and "The Designated Student" in Appendix I of the present volume, and compare Sorenson [1982].

G. E. Moore considered that it was paradoxical for me to assert "*p*, but I do not believe that *p*," despite the fact that the quoted sentence is consistent and, indeed, the fact it expresses might be true of me. (E.g., you could truly say of me: "*p*, but he does not believe it.") This may be connected with the Unexpected Examination: See Wright and Sudbury [1977].

Burge [1984] provides a very rich comparison between the Knower and the Liar.

5.   CLASSES AND TRUTH

The paradoxes to be discussed in this chapter are probably the hardest of all, but also the most fecund. Russell's paradox about classes, which he discovered in 1901, produced an enormous amount of work in the foundations of mathematics.[1] Russell thought that this paradox was of a kind with the paradox of the Liar, which in its simplest form consists in the assertion "I am now (hereby!) lying." The Liar Paradox has been of the utmost importance in theories of truth. Everything to do with these paradoxes is highly controversial, including whether Russell was right in thinking that his paradox about classes and the Liar Paradox spring from the same source (see section 5.3).

5.1.   RUSSELL'S PARADOX

If Socrates is a man, then he is a member of the class of men. If he is a member of the class of men, then he is a man. Can *classes* be members of classes? The answer would seem to be Yes. The class of men has more than 100 members, so the class of men is a member of the class of classes with more than 100 members. By contrast, the class of the Muses does not belong to the class of classes having more than 100 members, for tradition has it that the class of Muses has just twelve members.

Most classes are not members of themselves. The class of men is a class and not a man, so it is not a member of the class of men, that is, not a member of itself. However, some classes are members of themselves: The class of all classes presumably is, and so is the class of all classes with more than 100 members. So is the class of nonmen: the class of all and only those things that are not men. Since no class is

---

[1]   His first public account of this paradox appeared in Russell [1903]. For an overview, see van Heijenoort [1967].

a man, the class of nonmen is not a man, and thus meets the condition for itself being a member of the class of nonmen.

Consider the class of all classes that are not members of themselves. Let us call this class R. The necessary and sufficient condition for something to belong to R is that it be a class that is not a member of itself. Question: Is R a member of itself?

Suppose that it is. Then R must meet the (necessary) condition for belonging to R: that it is not a member of itself. So if it is a member of itself, it is not a member of itself.

Suppose that it is not. Then, being a non-self-membered class, it meets the (sufficient) condition for belonging to R: that it is not a member of itself. So if it is not a member of itself, it is a member of itself.

Summarizing: R is a member of itself if and only if it is not a member of itself. This is a contradiction.[2]

To have a contradiction is not necessarily to have a paradox. Recall the Barber Paradox from the Introduction. The barber shaves all and only those who do not shave themselves. Who shaves the barber? By reasoning similar to that used to derive Russell's Paradox, we find that the barber shaves himself if and only if he does not – a contradiction.

We respond to the Barber Paradox simply by saying that there is no such barber. Why should we not respond to Russell's Paradox simply by saying that there is no such class as R? The difference is this: Nothing leads us to suppose that there is such a barber; but our understanding of classes makes it very natural to suppose that there is such a class as R. Of course, we are forced by the paradox to accept that there cannot be such a class. This is paradoxical because it shows that some very compelling views about what it is for a class to exist have to be abandoned.

2

The Class Paradox, as Russell saw, is very similar to one that concerns properties. Most properties are not applicable to themselves. The property of being a man is a property and not a man, so it does not apply to the property of being a man; that is, it is not self-applicable. However, some properties are self-applicable: The property of being a property presumably is, and so is the property of being a property true of more than 100 things; etc.

Q: How would you spell out the contradiction?

The first paragraph of this section was supposed to introduce the natural or intuitive view of classes, which I must now make more explicit. I said that if Socrates *is a man,* then he is a member of the class of men. Let us use "condition" for what is expressed by, for example, the italicized phrase just used. Thus being a man is a condition, and one that Socrates satisfies, although Mont Blanc does not. The natural view of classes includes this principle of Class Existence:

> **CE.** To every intelligible condition there corresponds a class: Its members (if any) are all and only the things that satisfy the condition.

Corresponding to the condition of being a man, there is the class of men. Even when a condition is contradictory – for example, the condition of being both square and not square – there corresponds a class; though since nothing meets the condition, this is a class with no members (the "null" class).

CE appears to lead to Russell's Paradox. It entails that there is such a class as R if there is the intelligible condition: being a class that is not a member of itself. Yet we have already seen that there cannot be such a class as R.

We could put this point in a more symbolic and more perspicuous way as follows. Let us use "$\in$" to abbreviate "is a member of" (and "belongs to").

> **CE.** For every intelligible condition F, there is a class x, such that: For any object y, $y \in x$ if and only if y satisfies F.

For "y satisfies F" we can write, simply, "y is F"; for "if and only if" we can write "iff." Putting "R" for Russell's paradoxical class, "$\neg$" for "not," and "$\neg$ a member of itself" for "F, " CE yields:

> For any object y $y \in R$ iff $\neg(y$ is a member of itself).

What holds for anything must hold for R, so we get:

> $R \in R$ iff $\neg(R$ is a member of itself).

Since what it is for R to be a member of itself is for it to be a member of R, this yields the explicitly contradictory:

> **RP.** $R \in R$ iff $\neg(R \in R)$.

A natural suggestion at this point is that the condition is not genuinely intelligible – and this is, in effect, what most responses to Russell's Paradox suggest. If we follow this suggestion, CE can be preserved, as long as we take a sufficiently narrow view about what constitutes a condition. It must be stressed, however, that *if* we are also to preserve some well-known results in mathematics, it is far from obvious what this narrower view ought to be. In particular, reasoning and assumptions very like those that occur in the derivation of Russell's Paradox also occur in a famous proof by Cantor, which I shall now set out. Indeed, it was studying Cantor's proof that led Russell to the discovery of the paradox. It is very hard to see how to block the paradox while allowing the proof.

What is to be proved is that the power set of any class has more members than the class.[3] Cantor's proof could be sketched informally as follows:

1.   A class must have *at least* as many subclasses as members, since for each member the unit class to which it alone belongs is a subclass.
2.   So either there are as many subclasses as members or more.
3.   Suppose there are as many. This means that there is a

---

[3]   I am using "set" and "class" interchangeably. However, current usage confines "set" to only some and not all classes – intuitively, a set is a well-behaved class.

The *power set* of a class is the class consisting of every subclass of the class. Consider, for example, the class consisting of just the three elements *a, b*, and *c*, which we can write {*a,b,c*}. A class α is a subclass of a class β if and only if every member of α is a member of β. The class {a,b,c} has the following subclasses: (1) Λ (the null class) – since Λ has no members, every member of Λ is a member of {a,b,c}; (2) {a}; (3) {b}; (4) {c}; (5) {a,b}; (6) {a,c}; (7) {b,c}; and (8) {a,b,c} – since each member of this class is a member of {a,b,c}.

There are thus eight subclasses of a class with three members. So the class of all subclasses of {a,b,c} is more numerous (by five members) than {a,b,c} itself. Cantor's theorem holds obviously for classes with finitely many members. The interest of the theorem consists in the fact that it applies to classes of every cardinality.

A one–one function between two classes, α and β, associates each member of α with exactly one member of β, and each member of β with exactly one member of α. Cantor adopts the convention that two classes have the same number of members (the same cardinality) if and only if there is a one–one function between them.

one–one function f correlating members of the class with its subclasses.

4. Now form the following subclass S: $x \in S$ iff $\neg[x \in f(x)]$. By the supposition at (3), for some α, $S = f(\alpha)$. Applying the definition of S we get

$\alpha \in S$ iff $\neg[\alpha \in f(\alpha)]$

Therefore, given $S = f(\alpha)$:

*$\alpha \in S$ iff $\neg(\alpha \in S)$.

5. This contradiction shows that we must reject the supposition at (3). Hence we must adopt the other alternative available in (2): A class has more subclasses than members.

In (4) we have a contradiction just like that involved in Russell's Paradox (compare the asterisked line with RP), but here used to serious and informative effect in the proof. Notice that the proof assumes that *if* there is a function f, then there is a subclass S. If we are to use the current suggestion that an overliberal interpretation of CE is to blame for the paradox, and yet preserve Cantor's proof, we need to find a restriction on the notion of a *condition* that allows, via CE, the hypothetical existence of the class S but disallows the existence of R. Moreover, to be philosophically satisfying, there must be a philosophical justification for the restriction, enabling us to understand the origin of the paradox and to feel that we have something better than an ad hoc blocking maneuver. It is to Russell's credit that he attempted to provide precisely this in his Vicious Circle Principle (VCP). His idea is that the condition involved in the specification of R is viciously circular, and therefore not intelligible. He thought that the VCP also explained away a number of other paradoxes including, most important, the Liar Paradox. Therefore, I shall discuss the VCP (in section 5.3) only after describing the Liar (in section 5.2).

The kind of philosophical explanation I have said we need is not the only approach to Russell's Paradox. For certain purposes, we can make ad hoc restrictions that leave enough of the theory of classes for the need in hand, but attempt no philosophical explanation of the restrictions. One popular approach along these lines involves seeing classes as arranged in a hierarchy, one that ensures that every class is on a higher level than any of its members. One's theory might ensure that no class belongs to itself: No expression of the form $x \in x$

would count as true. Alternatively, the language in which the theory is couched might contain no provision even for expressing the thought that a class is, or is not, self-membered: Expressions of the form $x \in x$ might be barred from counting as sentences of the language. From the philosophical point of view, however, we need not so much a workable and apparently consistent formal theory, but rather an informal understanding of the source of the paradoxes, and a justification for any restrictions that might be placed upon intuitively acceptable principles such as CE.

5.2.   THE LIAR

The material of this section is hazardous. (Recall the fate of Philetas, mentioned in the Introduction.)

A relatively recent version of the Liar Paradox appears in St. Paul's epistle to Titus (1, xii–xiii).[4] This version involves the notion of lying, and lying involves an intention to deceive. This feature is irrelevant to the paradox. Eliminating such irrelevancies, we get something like this:

What I am now saying is false.

The simplest version of all, which will be the starting point of the discussion, is

L_1. L_1 is false.

Here we have a sentence called L_1 that says of itself that it is false. Suppose it is true; then it is as it says it is – false. So it is false. However, suppose that it is false. Well, *false* is just what it says it is, and a sentence that tells it the way it is is true. So it is true. To sum up: If L_1 is true, it is false; and if it is false, it is true.

4

It is not clear that the saint sees any logical, as opposed to moral, problems. The relevant text is as follows:

12.   One of themselves, even a prophet of their own, said, The Cretans are always liars, evil beasts, slow bellies.
13.   This witness is true. Wherefore rebuke them sharply, that they may be sound in the faith.

Q: St. Paul's version depends on the assumption that all the other Cretans were liars. Construct an explicit argument for the contradiction (perhaps modeled on that given below for L_1) that makes this dependence plain.

Is this paradoxical? Perhaps it sounds as if it is, but let us examine it more carefully. We have two conditional claims:

(a) If L_1 is true, then it is false.
(b) If L_1 is false, then it is true.

We assume that anything that is false is not true, and anything that is true is not false; so (a) and (b) yield:

(a´) If L_1 is true, then it is not true.
(b´) If L_1 is false, then it is not false.

There is a principle of reasoning that the ancients called *consequentia mirabilis*.[5] The principle is that if something implies its own negation, then we can infer that negation. Both (a´) and (b´) offer inputs to this principle. The first assures us that "L_1 is true" implies its negation, so the principle tells us that we can infer that L_1 is not true. The second, in an exactly parallel way, enables us to infer that L_1 is not false. So standard reasoning guarantees that L_1 is not true and is also not false. Let us summarize this as follows:

G1. L_1 is neither true nor false.

Is *this* paradoxical? Not unless some *principle of bivalence* is true, a principle that says, roughly, that every sentence is either true or false. Otherwise we can simply *accept* (G1): We simply say that L_1 lies in a *gap* between truth and falsehood. This is an example of a "gap account" of the Liar Paradox (hence the "G" in G1).

Is any principle of bivalence true? The version given in the preceding paragraph is certainly not true. Questions are expressed in sentences, but no question is either true or false. Suppose then we restrict the principle to declarative, indicative sentences. Still, there are counterexamples. Consider this one:

You have stopped beating your wife.

If you have never beaten your wife, the sentence is certainly not true; but to say it is false suggests that you are still beating her. Again, consider a case in which someone says

That elephant is about to charge

---

[5] In a familiar notation, the principle expresses the truth functional validity of the sequent:

$$A \to \neg A \vdash \neg A$$

when there is no elephant in the offing. We certainly cannot count the
sentence as true; but can we count it as false? If we did this, should
not the following sentence be true?

> That elephant is *not* about to charge.

Yet, if there is no elephant, this seems as poor a candidate for truth as
the previous one.[6]

The intuitive belief to which the principle of bivalence is attempting
to give voice is that any nondefective representation of how things are
in the world must be either accurate or inaccurate, true or false.
However, there are various ways in which what purports to be a
representation may fail to represent – of which the case of the missing
elephant is an example. This is the category to which the gap theorist
consigns L_1. What is called for, however, is a more detailed account
of the conditions under which a purported representation is defective.

A gesture toward part of such an account could begin as follows.
Imagine a man who understands most of English, but not the word
"true." You could try to explain the notion of truth to him using the
following recipe:

> You should call a sentence true iff you are willing to assert it.

("Iff" abbreviates "if and only if.") The learner could use this explanation to respond to, for example, "Snow is white" by saying "True!",
and to respond to "Grass is red" by saying "Not true!" However, he
could not in the first instance use the explanation to find out how to
respond to a sentence like this one:

1.   "Snow is white" is true.

---

6   The theory of degrees of truth (see section 2.3) is, of course, a departure
from bivalence, though not of a kind that has any bearing on the present
discussion. A gap between values is not the same as an intermediate
value.

The arguments about bivalence presented here are extremely sketchy,
and fail to do justice to the complexity of the issue. In much recent
work, the notion of a proposition (or thought) has been asked to play
three different roles: (a) that to which truth and falsehood are properly
ascribed; (b) the meaning of sentences; (c) the content of "propositional
attitudes" like knowing and believing. The first role may push one
towards bivalence for propositions; the second role may pull the other
way. It is open to question whether a single entity can play all three
roles. The issue is too complex for discussion here, though it is relevant
to the paradoxes: see Burge [1984], esp. p. 10ff.

Until he has already understood "true," he cannot know what it would be to be willing use this sentence to assert something. At a later stage, once he becomes aware that he is to respond with "True" to "Snow is white," he will be able to see that he should assent to (1), and hence see that (1) is itself something to which "true" applies. One forms the picture of someone climbing a ladder: At the base there are sentences not containing the word "true," to which he can learn to apply the word. As he does so, he can thereby come to see how to apply the word to sentences such as (1) on the next rung up; sentences applying "true" to sentences at the base. He can work his way up this ladder indefinitely. Where S is a sentence not containing "true," he can use this process to understand any sentence of the form

> ... "S is true" ... is true,

where the second ellipsis stands in for any number of further occurrences of "is true."[7]

Learning how to apply the concept of truth requires there to be sentences that do not themselves invoke this concept: the *base* sentences. The learning situation mirrors a putative metaphysical fact: that *truth depends on something outside itself.* The gap theorist could say that sentences ascribing truth will themselves be true or false, that is, will be nondefective representations, only if they respect this fact. Let me try to explain this.

Whether or not "Snow is white" is true depends on whether or not snow is white. So in this simple case, whether or not something is true depends quite directly on a fact that can be expressed without invoking the concept of truth: on whether or not snow is white. This is an example of what I mean by saying that truth depends upon something outside itself. In more complex cases, the dependence is less direct. For example, consider (1) again. Whether (1) is true depends on whether or not "Snow is white" is true. This is turn depends on whether or not snow is white. So whether or not (1) is true depends, but at one remove, on whether or not snow is white. In the end, we get back to a non–truth-involving question. In this reflection, we travel down the ladder toward the base; in considering learning, we were traveling upward from the base – same ladder, different direction.

---

7   The first ellipsis indicates where an appropriate number of opening quotation marks should be inserted.

You get a falsehood by negating a truth.[8] This gives rise to a similar structure: For "Grass is green" to be false would be for "Grass is not green" to be true, which in turn would be for grass not to be green. Likewise, for "'Grass is green' is false" to be false would be for "'Grass is green' is not false" to be true, that is, for "Grass is green" not to be false, that is, for grass not to be green.[9] Like truth, falsehood requires contact with the ground – with facts not involving truth or falsehood.

To reinforce the suggestion, consider this series of sentences:

2.　　(1) is true.
3.　　(2) is true.
4.　　(3) is true.

...

Can we genuinely make sense of such a series? Everything depends upon what (1) is. If it is, for example, "Snow is white," then there is no problem: We reach base. However, we would never reach base if (1) were, for example,

1.　　(4) is true.

Here truth wanders in a circle, without ever touching the ground. In this case we need to say that none of the sentences is true – and also, for the same reason, none is false.[10]

This line of thinking gives a general explanation for accepting (G1): the view that L_1 is neither true nor false. It is neither true nor false because there is no reaching base: There is no getting to a non–truth-involving fact on which the truth or falsehood of L_1 could depend. We come back always to L_1 itself, which is not a base sentence. To summarize: The trouble with L_1 is that it is *ungrounded*.

---

[8]　For this discussion, I am pretending – strictly incorrectly – that negation is symmetric, so that not only is

Grass is not green

a negation of

Grass is green

but the latter is also a negation of the former.

[9]　There is oversimplification here: A sentence might fail to be false without its negation being true. That is precisely what is being claimed for "ungrounded" sentences such as L_1.

[10]　The discussion is drawn from Kripke [1975].

The same account also applies well to

T$_1$.   T$_1$ is true.

Here is a sentence that says of itself that it is true. It is not paradoxical: The supposition that it is true does not lead to the conclusion that it is not; the supposition that it is not true does not lead to the conclusion that it is. Still, intuitively there is something wrong with T$_1$, the same sort of thing that is wrong with L$_1$. The account just given identifies the problem: T$_1$ is ungrounded. Like L$_1$, it does not make contact with a non–truth-involving base, so both sentences are neither true nor false.

This suggested response faces a problem known as the Strengthened Liar. Consider the sentence

L$_2$.   L$_2$ is not true.

This is even more immediately paradoxical than L$_1$. Suppose L$_2$ is true. Then it is as it says it is, viz., not true; so it is not true. However, suppose that it is not true. Well, *not true* is just what it says it is, and a sentence that tells it the way it is is true; so it is true. To sum up: If L$_1$ is true, it is not true; if it is not true, it is true.[11]

Here we have, apparently, a genuine contradiction. For two reasons, there would seem to be no chance of accepting, on the lines of G1,

G2.   L$_2$ is neither true nor not true.

First, this appears to be a contradiction: Standard reasoning would enable us to infer from G2 that L$_2$ is both true *and* not true.[12] Second, G2 implies quite directly that L$_2$ is not true (for anything that is *neither* φ *nor* ψ is certainly not φ), and this leads us back to the original problem: If it is not true, then it is.

I shall later show how a thought along the lines of G2 can be revived. First, I shall introduce a different line of response to L$_1$ and

---

[11]   Q*: Show that, on plausible assumptions, one can derive a genuine contradiction from L$_1$: viz., that L$_1$ is false, and also is not false. What assumptions does your argument require?

[12]   The reasoning depends on the equivalence between

neither *P* nor *Q*

and

both not-*P* and not-*Q*.

L_2. This is the "hierarchy of levels" account of truth. It comes in various forms, and stems from Tarski.

In deriving superficially unacceptable conclusions from L_1 and L_2, we relied on two principles:

> that if a sentence is true, then things are as it says they are; and
>
> that if things are as a sentence says they are, then the sentence is true.

Tarski stressed this feature of truth, which he expressed in a somewhat formal way. Let us use σ to stand in for a name of any sentence, and p to stand in for a sentence. Then, Tarski claimed, for any acceptable language we must accept every instance of

T. σ is true iff p

provided that the sentence named by σ means the same as the sentence that replaces p.[13] In the limiting case, these can be the same sentence; so an instance of T (putting "'Snow is white'" for σ and "Snow is white" for p) is

"Snow is white" is true iff snow is white.

Instances of T may seem utterly platitudinous; but the Strengthened Liar shows that, on the contrary, there are contradictory instances of T. Putting "L_2" for σ and "L_2 is not true" for p, we get:

*L_2 is true iff L_2 is not true.

This is a way of stating the problem posed by the Liar. Tarski's response is that the ordinary concept of truth, the one we use every day, is incoherent and must be rejected. According to Tarski, it needs to be replaced by a series of concepts of truth, hierarchically arranged, and each expressed in a language different from any natural language (i.e., from any language that has evolved naturally). This is the famous "Tarski hierarchy."

Suppose a certain language λ_0 contains a predicate Tr_1 that applies to all and only the true sentences of λ_0. Suppose also that λ_0 contains a sentence σ that says of itself that it is not Tr_1. Then we have a version of the Liar: If Tr_1 applies to σ, then σ is true – in which case,

---

13   Tarski [1937], pp. 187–8; see also the bibliographical notes at the end of this chapter.

given what it says, Tr_1 does not apply to it; but if Tr_1 does not apply to it, then, since this is what is says, it is true, and so Tr_1 does apply to it. Tarski took the contradiction to refute the supposition that σ belongs to λ_0. The natural further conclusion is that Tr_1 is not an expression of λ_0. Hence, no sentence belongs to λ_0 if it contains Tr_1.[14] This clearly blocks the paradox.

We can enlarge a language by adding new expressions. In particular, we could enlarge λ_0 by adding Tr_1. We could call the newly formed language λ_1, and σ would belong to λ_1. However, there is still no paradox because, since σ does not belong to λ_0, and since Tr_1 is defined only for λ_0 sentences, there is no question of Tr_1 applying to σ.

It is not that there is no predicate true of just the sentences of λ_1. There is: Call it Tr_2. However, for by now familiar reasons, it cannot belong to λ_1.[15] In general, a predicate Tr_n cannot belong to a language λ_{n-1} but only to a language of level at least n.

As a response to the Liar, Tarski's hierarchy is radical. It involves the claim that our actual concept of truth is incoherent: We have to replace it by a family of new concepts, each fixed to a level in the hierarchy, in the way just described. Many people have sought something less radical, a response that preserves more of our ordinary thought and talk.

One such less radical response draws on a Tarskian notion of a hierarchy, but claims that this is already implicit in our actual use of "true." Unlike Tarski's account, which claimed that ordinary language is irremediably defective, this alternative claims that the defects are mere appearance: The underlying reality is that we already use a Tarski-like hierarchy of concepts of truth.

---

14   For a careful statement of Tarski's precise premises, together with a challenge to the full generality of the conclusion Tarski drew, see Gupta [1982], Sc. II.

For each truth predicate in the hierarchy, Tarski accepts every instance of T. The fact that T has an inconsistent instance, if instances can be formed from any grammatically acceptable construction of English – in particular L_2 – is taken to show that there is no such coherent language as English. Replacing the single English predicate "true" by a hierarchy of truth predicates also involved, in Tarski's eyes, doing away with English, as normally understood.

15   Q: How does the supposition that Tr_2 belongs to λ_1 lead to paradox?

A major difficulty with this suggestion is that there would appear to be nothing in our usage reflecting the appropriate sensitivity to Tarski-style, fixed-in-advance levels. For example, suppose I say:

What you said just now is not true.

On the face of it, anyone, including myself, could quite well know what I have said without knowing what you have said. (Imagine a game on the lines of paper, stone, and scissors: I have to guess whether what you have just written down is true or false.) On a hierarchical view in which levels are fixed in advance, something in my use of this sentence determines an association between "true" and some level. Presumably the normal (default) level would be 1. If you have said "Snow is white," there is no problem; but suppose you have said "What M. S. will say is true." On the present theory, the intelligibility of my utterance requires my "true" to be on a higher level than yours; but if my utterance can be understood without knowing what you have said, its level of truth must get fixed independently of the content of what you have said. This means that the attempt to apply this kind of hierarchy response to natural language is extremely implausible.

Let us review the responses so far. We have mentioned the *gap response,* which holds that L_1 is neither true nor false; it has some difficulty in coping with L_2. We have Tarski's version of the *hierarchy response,* which is implausible because it involves jettisoning our ordinary concept of truth.   Finally, we have another version of the hierarchy response, which claims to find in ordinary language a Tarski-like hierarchy, but is implausible because there is no linguistic evidence for such a hierarchy. What other *kinds* of response are there?

Assuming that we cannot accept contradictions, there is only one kind left, as far as I know. This what I shall call the *syntactic response.* A particular and common version of this response dwells on the self-referential nature of L_1 and L_2: Each says something of itself. One might hold that such self-reference is unintelligible. The sentences afflicted by it have no literal meaning, and so cannot properly figure in any argument; hence they cannot lead to the paradoxical conclusion.

The general nature of this response is that one can tell, simply by inspecting how certain sentences, notably L_1 and L_2 are composed – by examining their syntax – that they are unintelligible. The trouble is that there are other versions of essentially the same paradox of which it is clear that this objection cannot be made. Imagine the following situation:

A   (said by α on Monday): Everything β will say on Tuesday is true.
B   (said by β on Tuesday): Nothing α said on Monday is true.
C   (said by γ on Tuesday): Nothing α said on Monday is true.

If α and β said nothing other than, respectively, (A) and (B) on, respectively, Monday and Tuesday, we have a paradox of essentially the Liar type. Suppose (B) is true; then (A) is not true, and β will say something not true on Tuesday. Since β only says (B), (B) is not true. So if (B) is true, then it is not true. Suppose (B) is not true; then α said something true on Monday. Since α only said (A), (A) is true, that is, everything β will say on Tuesday is true. This includes (B), so (B) is true. Thus if (B) is not true, it is true.

The reason for belaboring the point is this: The syntactic response has to say that either (A) or (B) or both are unintelligible. However, this is extremely implausible: There is no syntactic difference between (B) and (C); yet (C), even under these very circumstances, leads to no paradox. Furthermore, if β had not uttered (B), (C) would have been unproblematically true or false. What β says cannot affect the *syntax* of (C), so it is implausible to suggest that there is anything wrong with the syntax of (C). Hence, it is implausible to say that there is anything wrong with the syntax of (B).

Likewise, it is implausible to say that there is anything wrong with the syntax of (A) since, under other circumstances [in which β did not utter (B), for example], it would have raised no problems at all, led to no paradox, and been true or false, as the case may be.

So the syntactic response is, in general, unpromising because paradox can, in certain circumstances, beset a sentence that has a perfectly nonparadoxical use. Understanding a use of the sentence does not require of us sufficiently detailed knowledge of the circumstances to determine whether it is, in this use, paradoxical or not.

The particular version of the syntactic response that blames self-reference is even less promising, for two additional reasons. First, self-reference is essentially used in universally accepted theorems of logic and mathematics – for example, in Gödel's incompleteness theorem. Second, the heart of the paradox can be retained without self-reference, as we have already seen with α, β, and γ. There are simpler versions of the Liar without self-reference – for example, the piece of paper with only the sentence "What's on the other side of this paper is true" written on one side, and only "What's on the other side of this paper is false" written on the reverse.

I now return to the gap response, which I said had trouble with L_2. Let us build up to a way of attending to the problem by looking at a quite different application of the idea of a gap.

Some people hold that some predicates have a restricted significance range. For example, it might be held that a predicate like "hungry" can apply significantly only to living things. If Hugo is a living thing, then either applying the predicate "hungry" to him or denying the predicate of him will result in a true sentence: The application will be true if Hugo is hungry, the denial true if he is not. However, the doctrine continues, with respect to an inanimate object (e.g., this page), neither the application nor the denial of the predicate is true. The application is obviously not true. The claim is that the denial is also not true: If it were true, that could only be because this page had, for example, recently eaten, which it obviously has not. So the claim is that "hungry" applies significantly only to animate things: If you apply it to, or deny it of, anything else you get a sentence that is not true. Other examples of this doctrine would be the restriction of shape and color predicates to extended objects (so that, e.g., "triangular" does not apply significantly to any number), the restriction of mental state predicates to thinking things (so that, e.g., "is thinking of Vienna" does not apply significantly to a stone), and the restriction of arithmetic predicates to arithmetic objects (so that, e.g., "is prime" does not apply significantly to a tree).

For our purposes, it does not matter whether any of these specific doctrines is correct or not. What matters is their structure. The gap theorist, I suggest, will respond to L_2 by a doctrine structurally similar to the rather humdrum doctrines of the previous paragraph. Let us call this G3:

G3. "True" cannot be correctly applied to, nor denied of, L_2.

This contrasts with G2:

G2. L_2 is neither true nor not true.

G2 had the undesirable immediate consequence that L_2 is not true, and this allowed the paradoxical reasoning to the conclusion that it *is* true. G3, by contrast, does not have this as an *immediate* consequence, and is thus a promising version of the gap theory. Of course, a defense of the theory would require a justification for G3, and presumably this would take the form of arguing that the significance range of "true" is restricted to grounded sentences. I shall not pursue this aspect, but will return to the consideration of whether G3, if justifiable, would constitute an adequate response to the paradox.

When we ask what it is for "true" not to be correctly applicable to, or deniable of, a sentence, we find that paradox once again threatens. In general, for a predicate to be correctly applicable to an object entails the truth of a sentence formed by combining a name of the object with the predicate. (Thus, for "hungry" to be correctly applicable to Hugo, some sentence such as "Hugo is hungry" must be true.) For a predicate to be correctly deniable of an object entails the truth of a sentence formed by combining a name of the object with the negation of the predicate. (Thus, for "hungry" to be correctly deniable of Hugo, some sentence like "Hugo is not hungry" must be true.) G3 has it that "true" is not correctly deniable of L_2, and so it has it that a sentence formed by combining a name of the sentence with "not true" is not true. It thus entails that

"L_2 is not true" is not true.

However, L_2 is the sentence "L_2 is not true"; that is,

$L_2 = $ "L_2 is not true."

From these two premises we should be able to infer

L_2 is not true

simply by replacing one name of the sentence by another. From this we could go on to establish, by familiar reasoning, that L_2 is true. In other words, though less immediately than G2, G3 appears to entail the paradoxical L_2. Thus it does not by itself constitute an adequate response to the paradox.

In the remainder of this section, I shall suggest that the most promising response to the paradox combines some elements from the hierarchy response and others from the gap response. In particular, I shall argue that a correct understanding of the gap response shows that it is committed to adding some form of hierarchy response. To prepare the way for this position, I shall now describe a version of the hierarchy response that differs markedly from the two versions so far considered.

A common feature of the versions discussed is that they envisage fixed-in-advance levels. This is implausible because the level will be involved in determining which truth predicate we are dealing with; thus understanding the sentence would involve knowing what level is at stake. However, there seem to be examples in which we can plainly in some sense understand a sentence without knowing what level of truth is involved. If we could find a version of the hierarchy response that did not involve fixed-in-advance levels, perhaps it would provide an adequate response, either on its own, or in combination with a gap theory.

Tyler Burge [1979] has suggested a hierarchy response designed to avoid the standard objections to a Tarski-like hierarchy. Burge proposes that we regard "true" as genuinely a single truth predicate, though one that connects with levels *indexically*. Consider the word "I": We want to say that, in some sense of "meaning," it has a constant meaning, whoever uses it, despite having a different reference in different mouths. This is typical of indexical expressions. In the same way, the idea is that "true," though having a constant meaning, should relate to different levels depending on the context of its use. The value of this point is that it opens the way to the possibility of incorporating levels, though non-Tarskian ones, into an account of truth, yet avoiding the standard objections to Tarski's levels, regarded as an account of our ordinary notion of truth.[16]

Burge claims that the reasoning that seemed disasterous for our G3 can be analyzed as follows:

1. Familiar reasoning leads us to the conclusion that L_2 is true if and only if it is not true.
2. We then want to say that L_2 *is not true:* not because there are coherent conditions for its truth that it fails to meet, but rather to register the fact that there are no coherent conditions for its truth.
3. This then leads to the conclusion that L_2 *is true* after all, since it tells things the way they are – the way we have said they are in the italicized part of (2) above.

Burge suggests that we need not so much to repudiate this reasoning as to justify it. We can do this by seeing a shift of level indexically

---

[16] Here it must be stressed that Tarski did not intend his levels as an account of our ordinary notion of truth, which he thought was incoherent and thus insusceptible of theory.

triggered in the reasoning from (2) to (3). If we use "i" to subscript the level of the word "true" as it occurs in (2), then the italicized sentences in (2) and (3) are not in contradiction, since, fully written out they are

L_2 is not true$_i$

and

L_2 is true$_{i+1}$

These are no more in contradiction than are

I am hungry

and

I am not hungry

regarded as uttered by different people. Just as the consistency of the latter pair is secured by "I" having a different reference on each occasion, so the consistency of the former pair is secured by "true" relating to a different level on each occasion: level i on the first, level $i + 1$ on the second.

The reasoning from (1) to (3) can be diagnosed, says Burge, as follows. In the first stage we try to apply "true$_i$" to L_2, and in doing so we discover the contradiction. This leads us at (2) to deny this predicate of L_2. In the third stage we conclude that L_2 is true at a higher level.

Is the account adequate? A difficulty is posed by the fact that Burge accepts the result at stage (2) just as it stands, without invoking any difference of levels. On his view, we use "true$_i$" at this stage to say that there are no conditions, fixed by the meaning of L_2, that determine either that L_2 is true$_i$ or that it is not true$_i$. This is how, on Burge's view, we find ourselves committed to accepting the paradoxical sentence itself, as italicized in (2), even though, at this stage, we are trying to deny that the sentence has truth conditions. Whereas some responses try to show that there is not really any such commitment, Burge says that in this case appearance does not deceive: We really must accept everything in (2).

Let us, then, compare Burge's position with an alternative that repudiates the apparent acceptance of L_2 in (2). First, I shall discuss two questions that an adherent of such a position might address to Burge; then I shall field an example of the position itself.

Burge's acceptance of the stage (2) utterance of L_2, interpreted as having the same level of truth as at its stage (1) utterance, raises these two questions:

1.   What blocks the familiar reasoning from the assertion of L_2 at stage (2) to the contradictory conclusion that L_2 is $true_i$?
2.   Given that L_2 has no $truth_i$-conditions, how can it be correct to assert it?

The response to the first question is that the reasoning at stage (1) has already shown that a premise that would be needed to arrive at "L_2 is $true_i$" is unavailable. Informally, we might try to argue as follows: If, as we assert, L_2 *is not true$_i$*, then L_2 tells it as it is, and so *L_2 is true$_i$*. The bridge between the italicized sentences is supposedly provided by a level-relative instance of T:

σ is $true_i$ iff p.

Putting "L_2" for σ and "L_2 is not $true_i$" for p,

L_2 is $true_i$ iff L_2 is not $true_i$.

The idea would be that we apply our assertion at stage (2) of the right-hand side of the biconditional to derive the left-hand side. However, what the earlier reasoning showed was that L_2 had no coherent $truth_i$-conditions: The relevant instance of T is contradictory. Hence the reasoning to "L_2 is $true_i$" is not sound.

The reasoning at the first stage had, explicitly or implicitly, a different structure: that of *reductio ad absurdum* of the supposition that L_2 has coherent $truth_i$-conditions. The threatened reasoning at the second stage attempts to wrench out of context a strand from the first stage. In the first stage, *L_2 is not true$_i$* was a supposition used in the *reductio,* whereas in the second stage it is available categorically. What prevents paradox is the fact that other elements in the first stage of the reasoning having the status of suppositions are not available categorically at the second stage. Indeed, the relevant supposition has, by then, the status of a refuted hypothesis.

Turning to the second question, when levels are not at issue the obvious connection between acceptance and truth is simple: One should accept what is true. The most immediate way to extend this to indexical levels would involve a single contextually determined level, and a rule to the effect that one should accept what is $true_k$, where k is the contextually determined level of truth currently in force. This simple rule, however, would identify level i as the level in force in connection with the utterance of L_2 at stage (2), for that is the level of truth involved in the assertion. According to this rule, it would be *incorrect* to accept L_2, since it is not true$_i$. What is needed is a twofold indexical determination of level: a determination of the level relevant to *interpretation,* which, at stage (2), is still level i; and a determination of the level relevant to *evaluation,* which, at stage (2), has to be j. The connection between acceptance and truth is that one should accept what is true$_k$, where k is the contextually determined level of *evaluation* currently in force. Hence one should accept L_2 as uttered at stage (2), though not as uttered at stage (1). It seems to me that whether a justified account of this twofold determination can be given is open to question,[17] and that it is therefore worth exploring an alternative view: one upon which the utterance at stage (2) is regarded as acceptable only in virtue of exploiting a higher level of truth in its *interpretation.*

It is very easy to state the main point of one suggestion along these lines: You cannot specify gaps (of the kind in question) without introducing a hierarchy of levels. If this is true, it would very satisfactorily motivate the gap plus hierarchy response to the Liar Paradox.

Let us go back to the humdrum examples of gap theories, like the one that says "hungry" is significantly applicable only to living things. This entails, for example, that:

H.   "This piece of paper is hungry" is not true, and "This piece of paper is not hungry" is not true.

It is not that these quoted sentences are unintelligible or nonsensical, but merely that they are neither of them true.[18]   We cannot express H

---

[17]   But see the mention of Robert Koons in the bibliographical notes.

[18]   Intelligibility is thus a broader notion than significance, if the latter involves having a truth condition. It is essential to the gap response, as I understand it, that it should allow a threefold classification of sentences: those that are completely successful, which will be true or false; those that are, as I call it, intelligible (we can see what they are driving at), but that fail to be true because, e.g., the subject lies outside the significance range of the predicate; and finally nonsense. Reverting to the α, β, γ version of the paradox, the gap theorist must allow that (B) is *intelligible* even if α says what he does. (A) deprives (B) of a truth condition ("significance") but not of intelligibility, and the sense of "understanding" in which we want to say that we can understand (B) despite (A) must relate to intelligibility, in the first instance, rather than to significance.

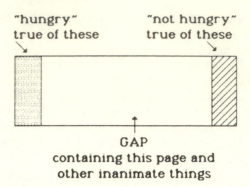

Figure 5.1. Geometric representation of H: "This piece of paper is hungry" is not true, and "This piece of paper is not hungry" is not true.

by saying "This piece of paper is neither hungry nor not hungry" (compare G2), for this would entail "This piece of paper is not hungry," which is just the sort of thing we *do not* want to say.

This piece of paper falls into the gap with respect to "hungry" (or so we are pretending). The use of the word "gap" here comes from a geometric representation of facts like H. Suppose that we represent all the things there are by the outer rectangle in Figure 5.1, the things of which "hungry" is true by the gray area at the left, and the things of which "not hungry" is true by the hatched area at the right. There is a gap between these areas, a gap containing this piece of paper and other inanimate things.

I want to suggest that there is no way of using, but not mentioning, "hungry" and yet expressing this fact of "gappiness." We have already seen that "This piece of paper is neither hungry nor not hungry" will not do, and we can argue quite generally that there is *no* way of doing it: for if we are to *use* (as opposed to mention) "hungry," we must use it *of* something. Of what shall we use it? Not, by hypothesis, of this piece of paper; but it is impossible to see how using it of anything else could say what is needed concerning *this piece of paper*. Moreover, I cannot see that anything hinges on the choice of example. It seems to be generally true that if we want to say that an object falls into a gap with respect to a predicate, we cannot use that predicate to say so. I am going to call this "the principle." I shall return later to an objection to it. Before doing so, I want to show how neatly its truth would motivate superimposing levels on gaps as a response to the Liar.

Return to L_2 and consider the task of saying that it falls in the gap with respect to "true" (cf. saying that this piece of paper falls in the gap with respect to "hungry"). Applying the principle, we find that we cannot use the predicate "true" to say this. Let us distinguish the predicate we *use* to assign L_2 to its gap by writing it in small capitals. We know that we want to say the following [compare this with (H)]:

S.   "L_2 is true" is not TRUE and "L_2 is not true" is not TRUE.

Question: "true" = "TRUE"? Applying the principle, the answer has to be no. Since "TRUE" is *used* in S to assign an object (viz., L_2) to a gap with respect to "true," it cannot be identical with the predicate "true"; for the principle has it that you cannot use a predicate to say of an object that it falls into a gap with respect to that same predicate.[19] The upshot is, on this approach, that we cannot accept (2) in the reasoning set out above.

Different as "true" and "TRUE" may be, they are evidently closely related, and a full story would spell out just what their relations are. Since there will be a seemingly paradoxical sentence like L_2 but with "TRUE" in place of "true," there will be a series of different predicates. Clearly the situation is ripe for a levels approach; and if they could be indexically triggered levels, we could have them without abandoning the essential unity of truth.

There are many different objections that may be made to this suggestion – so many that I cannot begin to speak to all of them. I shall choose just one. This objection concerns the principle that if an object falls into a gap with respect to a predicate, this fact cannot be expressed by using the predicate. However, suppose there were a negationlike operator φ, with truth conditions that ensure that

⌜$\varphi(A)$⌝ is to be asserted iff ⌜A⌝ is not to be asserted.[20]

---

[19]   This is where the difference between the present suggestion and Burge's is at its sharpest. In saying that at stage (2) we recognize that L_2 has no truth$_i$ conditions, Burge is in effect saying that L_2 falls into a truth$_i$ value gap. If what I call "the principle" is correct, he cannot express this, as he attempts to do, by using "true$_i$."

[20]   The effect of the corner quotes (⌜ , ⌝) is to enable one to read the above as: "Any expression prefaced by an occurrence of 'φ' is to be asserted iff the expression itself is not to be asserted."

Then one could properly assert:

$\varphi(L_2$ is true$)$ and $\varphi(L_2$ is not true$)$.

The gap with respect to "true" would have been expressed *using* "true" (for "true" is the *only* predicate used). Moreover, we can apparently easily state a truth condition that would yield the desired assertion condition. Suppose our logic is three-valued, with a third value to represent the gap between truth and falsehood. Then φ could be a truth-functional operator that maps truth onto falsehood and everything else onto truth.

I have to maintain that this is incoherent. My ground is that no operator could yield as output a sentence not in the gap if the input sentence is in the gap. My ground for this, in turn, is that to be in the gap is to suffer a semantic defect that will be inherited by any operation. To be in the gap is to lack a truth condition, so being in the gap is being unavailable as an argument to a truth function. Being in the gap is not having another, different sort of truth value from the values true and false, but rather being incapacitated from saying anything, or contributing, in use, to the saying of anything. This is the explanation of what I earlier called "the principle."

So, the principle stands: You cannot use a predicate to express the fact that an object falls into a gap with respect to it. If this is correct, then Burge is wrong to accept what is stated in (2); though a correct response will no doubt draw upon his idea of indexically triggered levels.

This is only the outline of a suggested response to the Liar: a response that combines gaps and a hierarchy of levels. A full working out would require much else, notably a justification for G3 *other* than the mere fact that it helps to avoid paradox, and an account of how the levels are determined. I shall not attempt these tasks, but will instead return to the question, raised in section 5.1, of whether the paradoxes of classes and truth considered in this chapter are species of a common genus, as Russell maintained.

5.3.   THE VICIOUS CIRCLE PRINCIPLE

Are the two paradoxes of this chapter totally different, or essentially the same? Is the truth perhaps somewhere between these extremes?

One reason for thinking that they are similar is that the Class Paradox resembles a paradox about properties, and the Property Paradox in turn resembles the Liar. Most properties are not true of themselves: For example, the property of being a man is not true of itself, since that property lacks the property of being a man; but the property of being a nonman is true of itself, since the property of being a nonman has the property of being a nonman. The pattern of reasoning used in the case of the Class Paradox would lead to the conclusion:

> The property of *being not true of itself* is true of itself if and only if it is not true of itself.

There is at least a surface similarity between this contradiction and the contradiction that L_2 truly predicates truth of itself if and only if it does not. Where the Property contradiction uses the notion of *not true of,* a relation that may hold between a property and something else (perhaps also a property), the Liar contradiction uses the notion of *not true,* a property that a sentence may possess.

A second similarity is that both the Class Paradox and the Liar are usually stated in a way that involves self-reference, or something like it.

A third similarity concerns the use of CE and T in the derivation of the two paradoxes, and the roles of these principles in governing intuitive notions of *class* and *truth.*

On the side of derivation, the comparison is this: The schema

> for any object y, $y \in x$ iff y is F

yields a contradiction when x is replaced by a name, say R, for the Russell class, and F by the condition, expressed in terms of this name, that supposedly defines membership for that class, "$\neg\in R$." Similarly, the schema

> σ is true iff p

yields a contradiction when σ is replaced by a name, say L_2, for the Liar sentence, and p by the condition, expressed in terms of this name, that supposedly defines truth for that sentence, "L_2 is not true."

On the side of roles, the comparison is that just as CE appears constitutive of our pretheoretical notion of a class, so T appears constitutive of our pretheoretical notion of truth. CE determines what it is for a class to exist; T determines what it is for a truth condition to exist.

A fourth surface similarity between the Class Paradox and the Liar is that hierarchies have been used in response to both kinds of paradox, beginning with one of the the earliest systematic treatments, in Russell [1908].

A contrasting view was proposed by Ramsey, who distinguished the Logical Paradoxes, under which heading he included the Class Paradox, from the Semantic Paradoxes, under which he included the Liar. Ramsey's distinction is based on which concepts appear essentially in the paradoxes: Truth – a semantic concept – appears essentially in the Liar, but not in the Class Paradox. Class membership – which Ramsey called a logical concept – appears essentially in the Class Paradox but not in the Liar.

Russell argued that both kinds of paradox – Class Paradoxes and Liar Paradoxes – have a common origin. This is not directly inconsistent with Ramsey's position. It could be that groups of paradoxes are in some respects dissimilar (for example, they contain different concepts essentially) while being in other respects similar (for example, they have common structural features – self-reference, perhaps).

Russell's classification of the Class Paradox and the Liar as of a common kind is based on the claim that they both alike derive from an infringement of what he called the Vicious Circle Principle (VCP). He gives more than one account of what the principle is, but a fair statement (not a quotation) would be as follows:

> No totality can contain members definable only in terms of itself.[21]

How can this rather mysterious principle be applied to the Class Paradox? The *definition* of the class R, of non-self-membered classes went like this:

> For any class x, $x \in R$ iff $\neg x \in x$.

The important point is that the definition speaks of what Russell would call a totality: the totality of all classes, introduced by the phrase "any class." Russell takes it that this is the only possible definition of R, and intends that the VCP tell us that R cannot belong to the totality introduced by the phrase "any class," as that occurs in the definition of

---

21 The formulation is verbally closest to Russell [1908], p. 75. The justification for "definable only" instead of the "defined" used at that point comes from the formulation at p. 63 of that work, and again in [1910], p. 37.

R. For suppose *R* did belong to that totality; then the totality would contain a member *R* definable only in terms of that totality, which is what the VCP says is impossible. However, if *R* does not belong to the totality introduced by "any class," then we cannot make the usual move to the contradiction. The usual move goes like this: If the definition holds of *any class*, then in particular it holds of *R*, so we can infer

$$R \in R \text{ iff } \neg R \in R.$$

The VCP has it that the totality introduced by *any class* excludes *R*, so this reasoning is fallacious. In effect, the upshot of the VCP is that we cannot define *R* as we had originally intended – in such a way, that is, that the question could arise about whether it has or lacks its defining property.

How does the VCP deal with the Liar? Russell does not entirely explicitly forge the connection. He first claims that the VCP establishes a hierarchy of propositions, and then claims that it follows from the hierarchy that no proposition can speak of itself. It might be better, and it is certainly more direct, to argue as follows. Suppose a proposition *A* involves reference to some totality of propositions *B*. Then *A* can only be defined (i.e., fully specified) in terms of this totality *B*. Then the VCP has it that *A* cannot belong to *B*. So, in particular, if *B* is a totality of one proposition, then a proposition cannot refer to itself.

An initial reaction, given the unproblematic quality of some forms of self-reference, is to say that if this argument is valid, it simply proves that the VCP is wrong. This response might be too swift: One would need to be sensitive to the difference between self-referential sentences and self-referential propositions.[22] Rather than pursue this

---

[22]   To see that there is a *prima facie* case for such a distinction, try constructing equivalents, in terms of propositions, of such unproblematic cases of sentential self-reference as

This sentence is written on a board in room 347.

There is no problem about identifying the sentence to which "this sentence" refers, since we can identify the sentence geometrically, and it is available to perception. Things are not the same with, for example, the following proposition:

This proposition is expressed by a sentence written on a board in room 347.

directly, I shall show that there is some connection between the guiding idea of the VCP and the notion of levels of truth. In conclusion, I shall see how one would have to think of classes, if this guiding idea is to apply to them too.

Suppose that a truth-ascribing proposition A' involves reference to some totality of propositions B'. Then A' can only be defined (i.e., fully specified) in terms of this totality B'. Then the VCP has it that A' cannot belong to B'; so no truth-ascribing proposition can ascribe truth to a truth-ascribing proposition (since to ascribe one must refer). We therefore get a twofold division, into propositions that are, and those that are not, truth-ascribing. If we in addition take seriously the apparent fact that we *can* ascribe truth to truth-ascribing propositions (e.g., "'Snow is white' is true" is true), we get a series of truth predicates in Tarski-style, each prevented, by a replication of the argument just given, from ascribing truth to a sentence containing itself. This hierarchy is visible in Russell [1908], the first presentation of his famous Theory of Types.[23]

The Theory of Types also appears to contain a hierarchy of classes.[24] The VCP might lead one to it by the reflection that, in specifying a class, one must not refer to, or presuppose, a totality of classes to which the class one is seeking to define would belong. Clearly, *one* way to achieve this is to insist that classes are arranged in a hierarchy of the following sort:

> at the base, nonclasses – *individuals,* as Russell called them;
> then classes all of whose members are individuals;

I am here thinking of a proposition as *what is said by a sentence.* It is an abstraction, not available to perception, and not describable geometrically. We cannot tell what the propositional content is until we know what proposition "this proposition" refers to, and we cannot know that until we know the propositional content expressed by the displayed sentence. There is, therefore, at least a *prima facie* case against the intelligibility of propositional as opposed to sentential self-reference.

[23] More exactly, the first presentation of the so-called "Ramified Theory of Types," which is now principally associated with Russell's name. Russell [1903], Appendix, contains a different theory of types.

[24] I say "*appears* to contain" because the theory of classes espoused at that time is called the "no-class" theory and is supposed to show us how to manage *without* having to assume that there are classes. If this is accepted literally, then the theory cannot *really* contain a hierarchy of classes.

then classes all of whose members are classes of individuals; and so on.

This is more controversial than the truth hierarchy, because it is so obvious that different hierarchies are possible, consistent with the VCP. For example, there seems no reason why the classes should not be "cumulative": Why should there not be classes containing both individuals and classes of individuals? If such a class does not also contain classes containing both individuals and classes of individuals, the VCP will have been honored.

One reason for doubting whether the VCP identifies a common feature of the Class Paradox and the Liar is that one can doubt whether it is true. Even if one accepts it, the maneuvering required to apply it to the Class Paradox is rather different from that required to apply it to the Liar; this diminishes the support it can lend to the similarity thesis.

Against the similarities must be weighed the dissimilarity between the concept of truth and the concept of a class. The former, thanks to its pervasive connections with our notions of correctness and acceptance, lies at the heart of our conception of language. The latter is much more limited in its application and not a distinctively semantic concept. The difference between them shows up in a number of ways. For example, the attempt to say that L_2 lacks truth conditions – to say that *there is no* sentence that genuinely says of itself that it is not true – apparently leads to the conclusion (the so-called Liar's Revenge) that L_2 is not true – for if it says nothing, it says nothing true. No such twist is consequent on the assertion that *there is no* such class as R. For the class paradox, it is clear what we need to say – that there is no class R – and unclear only how this can be justified. For the Liar, it is not clear even what ought to be said, let alone how it is to be justified.

The VCP suggests the thought that certain things, including classes and truth, are "derivative."[25] A class derives from its members, in the sense that it cannot exist unless its members do. An ascription of truth derives from the proposition to which it ascribes truth, in the sense that the ascription cannot exist unless the proposition does. Knowledge and belief derive from the proposition known, in the sense that there could not be such a thing as knowing something unless there were something to be known.

---

[25]   This usage comes from Burge [1978].

Compare the following nonparadoxical specifications of, in the first case, a class, and, in the other cases, propositions:

C_1. C is the class whose unique member is C.
T_1. T_1 is true.
K_1. You know that K_1.
B_1. You believe that B_1.

As far as I know, these do not lead to paradox; yet they are all plainly unsatisfactory, and for a similar sort of reason. In each case, we are trying to introduce a derived entity (class, proposition) yet in such a way as to exclude the provision of anything (member, other proposition) from which the derived entity can be derived. For T_1 what is lacking is what I earlier called "grounding." There is a similar kind of lack in the other cases.

This points to an explanation of why the paradoxes of Classes, the Liar, the Knower, and the Believer all suggest a hierarchy response. The hierarchy will reflect the facts of derivativeness: The underived things will be at the bottom (individuals, propositions not involving the notions of truth, knowledge, or belief, as the case may be). There should be no *a priori* expectation that the structure of the hierarchies will be the same: Classes may derive from their members differently from the ways in which some propositions derive from others; though one might surmise that the hierarchies relevant to the Liar, Knower, and Believer will be more similar to one another than any of them is to the Class hierarchy.

The suggestion, in short, is that a purely metaphysical notion – that of derivativeness – might be used to provide a philosophical justification both for a hierarchical conception of classes and for a hierarchical conception of propositions. Such a suggestion stands in need of a great deal of development, both technical and philosophical – but it has one merit that needs to be borne in mind when assessing any "solution" to paradoxes: It does provide some (purported) philosophical understanding of what is going on in the formation of the relevant paradoxes, and is not merely an ad hoc device to prevent their derivation.

BIBLIOGRAPHICAL NOTES

Tarski [1969] contains a semipopular exposition of his views. The classic text is Tarski [1937]; despite the technical nature of the main body of this piece, the first section is nontechnical, accessible, and well worth reading. He sets out a condition of adequacy for a formal definition of truth (symbolized "Tr"), called Convention T, as follows:

> A formally correct definition of the symbol "Tr" ... will be called an ... *adequate definition of truth* if it has the following consequences:
>
> (α) all sentences which are obtained from the expression "x ∈ Tr if and only if p" by substituting for the symbol "x" a structural-descriptive name of any sentence of the language in question and for the symbol "p" the expression which forms the translation of this sentence into the meta-language;
>
> (β) ... (pp. 187–8)

As it is sometimes put, Tarski allows us to draw on our intuitive conception of meaning (translation) in specifying the conditions for a correct definition of truth.

Prior [1961] should be read. There are some daunting formal parts in Polish notation but, even if these were taken on trust, the article would have a great deal to offer.

I borrow the word "grounding" and its cognates from Kripke [1975]. I do not claim to have captured what he means by it, for his concept of grounding is embedded in a mathematical theory to which I cannot begin to do justice. However, the early part of his paper is perfectly accessible to the nonmathematician and is to be read. A classic reference for grounding is Hertzberger [1970].

The expression "Strengthened Liar" is due to van Fraassen [1968], though the problem itself is much older.

For an excellent recent overview, see Martin's editorial Introduction [1984]. The collection in question contains some of the most important recent work on the subject, which includes lines of thought not mentioned in this chapter.

Ramsey's distinction between logical and semantic paradoxes is in his [1925], pp. 171–2.

The reliance on the principle of the substitutivity of identicals in section 5.2 is not uncontroversial. For example, Skyrms [1982] claims that the Liar Paradox shows that this principle is not correct. I happen to think that this position is extremely unintuitive: Cf. Burge [1979], p. 90.

In addition to the positive thesis of Burge [1979] – the statement of his view of the level-indexicality of truth – the paper contains extremely illuminating critical discussions of other positions, making it essential reading. Doubts of the kind mentioned earlier (at the citation of footnote 17 in section 5.2), if not already dispelled by Burge's own words, should be eliminated by recent unpublished work by Robert Koons, which came to my attention when the present book was already in press.

The generalization of the idea of grounding to that of derivativeness, mentioned at the very end, is due to Burge [1978]. He extends the suggestion in his important paper, "Epistemic paradox" [1984].

Barwise and Etchemendy [1987], published after the present book had gone to press, contains excellent discussions of the themes of this chapter and presents important work by Peter Aczel.

6. ARE ANY CONTRADICTIONS ACCEPTABLE?

The purpose of this chapter is to make explicit, and sketch a justification for, an assumption that I have made throughout: that contradictions are unacceptable. I have at many points argued that if something seems to lead to a contradiction, then either it, or the relevant reasoning, must be rejected. This assumption has come under attack at various times in the history of philosophy. Very recently, the attack has taken a subtle form and has harnessed impressive technical resources.[1]

Historically, one thing that has deterred many people from seriously entertaining the thought that a contradiction could be true is the classically valid inference rule: From a contradiction, anything may be derived. If this rule is accepted, then it would be crazy to believe a contradiction, for this would commit one to believing everything. Recently it has been shown that one can have a great deal of what one really wants from classical logic without accepting this rule. The result is that there can now be no knockdown argument against the view that a rational system of belief may contain a contradiction.

The version of this view that I shall consider derives from Graham Priest [1986]. He suggests that some contradictions, though not all, have the following three properties:

(a)   They are true (as well as being false).
(b)   They can be believed.
(c)   It can be rational to accept them.

I call the conjunction of these three views "dialetheism."[2]

---

[1]   See Rescher and Brandom [1980] and Priest, Routley, and Norman [1985].

[2]   Priest [1986] defines dialetheism by thesis (a).

141

Let me stress again that dialetheism accepts that all contradictions are false, so let us not push against that open door. What an opponent needs is an argument for the view that no contradictions are true. Here is a standard one. Contradictions have the form "A and not-A." "A" and "not-A" cannot both be true, given any notion of negation worthy of the name; and a conjunction one of whose conjuncts is not true cannot be true.

The dialetheist will deny both premises, so the argument will not persuade him. Let me concentrate on the first. He will say that "A" and "not-A" *can* both be true: They will be so precisely if "A" itself is false as well as true. To assume that "A" cannot be both true and false is simply to assume that dialetheism is false.

How could the dialetheist justify his account of negation? He will say that what matters are these uncontroversial principles:

N1. If A is true, then not-A is false.

N2. If A is false, then not-A is true.

Once we allow that there exists a sentence A that is both true and false, the principles simply entail that there exists a sentence such that both it and its negation are true.

If there are arguments that would refute dialetheism, they lie elsewhere. A promising area for examination is the role that the concepts of truth and falsehood play in our thinking; in particular, how they connect with acceptance and rejection. A standard view holds that these connections are as follows:

T.   If A is true, then it should be accepted.

F.   If A is false, then it should be rejected.

No state in which we can be constitutes the acceptance and rejection of a single proposition;[3] hence there is no state rationally appropriate to a proposition that is both true and false. In particular, it cannot be rational to believe something both true and false.

Priest accepts T but rejects F:

> Truth and falsity come inextricably intermingled. ... One cannot, therefore, accept all truths and reject all falsehoods ... (p. 106)

---

3   No *single* state, we might say, for, arguably, we all inadvertently on occasion are in the two states of believing A and also believing not-A. Priest takes it for granted that in arguing that some contradictions should be accepted he has to show that they should not also be rejected.

There has to be a sufficient condition for rejecting a proposition: Something about the way it relates to the world must make rejection the appropriate response. The dialetheist, who says that falsehood does not provide this sufficient condition, will presumably say that it is constituted by nontruth. Falsehood is a usually reliable sign, but not a guarantor, of nontruth. Propositions that are true and false are not nontrue, which is why rejection is not the appropriate response.

One might try the following argument for F. Since the negation of any falsehood is true, and since rejecting a proposition is accepting its negation, any falsehood must be rejected. Setting out the steps, the argument runs:

> A is false.
> Not-A is true   [by N2]
> Not-A is to be accepted.   [by T]
> A is to be rejected.

Priest holds that the move from the third to the fourth line is unwarranted. For suppose not-A is false (as well as true): Then A is true, and so to be accepted. It looks as if the argument for F turns on the presupposition of the falsity of dialetheism; yet this was what was to be proved.

In urging his point, Priest goes further than he needs. He suggests that there are intelligible states of mind that constitute the rejection of a proposition while not committing the subject to the acceptance of the proposition's negation. I am unconvinced that there could be such states.[4] However, this is beside the point; for as far as I can see, Priest can accept the inference from "A is to be rejected" to "not-A is true"; what he must reject is the converse. Certainly, rejecting this is enough to block the argument just considered.

A different line of objection to dialetheism is this. There is no room for an intelligible conception of falsehood that differs from nontruth. All our semantics, and a proper account of the conditions for rational belief, can be effected in terms of a single property, truth, which may

---

[4]   Priest's intuitionist, who, he claims, *rejects* an instance of the law of excluded middle should be seen as (perhaps stoutly or even vehemently) refusing to accept the instance. Refusing to accept is not the same as rejecting. Priest's statistician, who, he claims, rejects a *hypothesis,* resolving to spend no more time on it while having no evidence for, or inclination to accept, its negation, should be seen as rejecting from his agenda *the investigation of* the hypothesis.

be present or absent, but not both present and absent. To recognize its presence is to accept. To recognize its absence is to reject. To fail to recognize its presence and fail to recognize its absence is to be agnostic. Negation turns truth into nontruth, nontruth into truth. Conjunctions with nontrue conjuncts are nontrue. Nothing can be both true and nontrue. There is no room for dialetheism, since there is no room for a distinction between nontruth and falsity.

This attack invites an objection. We might want to say that a bowl of cherries lacks the property of truth. This alleged instance of nontruth is not a case of falsity; so the distinction between nontruth and falsity *is* needed, after all.

In response, it is proper to point out that this sort of case is not of the kind relevant to dialetheism. We beg no questions if we say, Let us restrict the discussion to genuine *propositions* (or whatever the preferred technical term may be): things, with no semantic defects, that succeed in representing some state of affairs. Concerning these, the attack against dialetheism holds. Either the represented state of affairs obtains or it does not. If it does, the proposition is true; if it does not, the proposition is not true. We can identify nontruth with falsehood, if we like; but there is simply no room for a *distinct* conception of falsehood. For propositions the possibilities are success (truth) and failure (nontruth), and there is no third possibility.

I think this achieves something. The dialetheist now has a debt to pay: He must justify the distinction between nontruth and falsehood. This means explaining how the distinction is required for purposes other than the defense of dialetheism. I believe, though I shall not attempt to show, that all extant attempts at providing this justification fail.

APPENDIX I

SOME MORE PARADOXES

(An asterisk before a title indicates that there is an observation on the entry in Appendix II.)

THE GALLOWS

The law of a certain land is that all who wish to enter the city are asked to state their business there. Those who reply truly are allowed to enter and depart in peace. Those who reply falsely are hanged. What should happen to the traveler who, when asked his business, replies, "I have come to be hanged"?

BURIDAN'S EIGHTH SOPHISM

Socrates in Troy says, "What Plato is now saying in Athens is false." At the same time, Plato in Athens says, "What Socrates is now saying in Troy is false." (Cf. Buridan, in Hughes [1982], pp. 73–9.)

THE LAWYER

Protagoras, teacher of lawyers, has this contract with pupils: "Pay me a fee if and only if you win your first case." One of his pupils, Euathlus, sues him for free tuition, arguing as follows: "If I win the case, then I win free tuition, as that is what I am suing for. If I lose, then my tuition is free anyway, since this is my first case."

Protagoras, in court, responds as follows: "If you give judgment *for* Euathlus, than he will owe me a fee, since it is his first case and that was our agreement; if you give judgment for me, then he will owe me a fee, since that is the content of the judgment."

145

THE DESIGNATED STUDENT

Five students are told by the teacher that all of them are to have a star pinned on their backs; that just one of the stars is gold – the recipient of this is the "designated student"; and that the designated student will not know he or she is designated. The students are lined up so that the fifth can see the backs of the other four, the fourth the backs of the other three, and so on.

They argue that what the teacher said cannot be true, for the following reasons:

> The fifth student can infer that he cannot be unknowingly designated, since, if he were designated, he could see, from the nongold nature of the stars on the other students, that none of them is designated, and thus could infer that he himself is designated.
>
> The fourth student can infer that (a) the fifth student cannot be unknowingly designated and (b) the fourth cannot be either, since, given that the fifth has not been designated, the fourth would be able to infer, from the nongold nature of the three visible backs, that he was designated, if he was.
>
> ... and so on.

Is this a genuine paradox? Is it a version of the Unexpected Examination? (See Sorenson [1982].)

*THE GRID

The following paradox has been said to be structurally like the Unexpected Examination. Is it? Does it contain a serious paradox?

In the Grid game, you are blindfolded and placed on a grid with numbered squares as shown in the diagram:

1	2	3
4	5	6
7	8	9

The heavy outer line represents a wall. You are allowed to move only horizontally or vertically, and you may attempt only two moves from your initial position. Your aim is to determine which square you are on. You might be lucky; for example, if you attempt a move right and feel the wall, then attempt a move down and feel the wall, you can infer that you are placed on square 9. However, you might be unlucky; for example, if you were placed on square 6 and moved left twice, you could not tell whether your initial position was 6, 3, or 9.

Suppose I claim that I can put you in an initial position not discoverable in two moves. However, you reason as follows: I cannot be put in any of the corner squares, since there are two-move sequences (like the one mentioned for square 9) that would tell me where I am; but if 1, 3, 7, and 9 can be eliminated, so can 2, 4, 6, and 8, since, for example, a move up into the wall would tell me that I was at 2, given the elimination of 1 and 3 as possibilities. Hence my initial position must be 5, and so I *can* discover my initial position – and in zero moves! (See Sorenson [1982].)

*THE STONE

Can an omnipotent being make a stone so heavy that he cannot lift it? He can, because, being omnipotent, he can do everything. However, he also cannot, since, if he could make it, there would be something he could *not* do – that is, lift it. (Reading: Savage [1967]; Schrader [1979].)

HETEROLOGICAL

Let us call an expression "heterological" if and only if it describes itself. Thus "short" is heterological because

"short" is short

is true; but "long" is not heterological since

"long" is long

is false.

Is "heterological" heterological or not?

We could shorten the definition to the following schema, abbreviating "heterological" as "het":

het("φ") iff $\neg\varphi$("φ").

The contradiction follows immediately by taking "het" as the replacement for the schematic φ. (Reading: Russell [1908]; Quine [1966]. esp. p. 4ff, "Grelling's Paradox.")

*THE LOTTERY

Suppose there are a thousand tickets in a lottery and only one prize. It is rational to believe of each ticket that it is very unlikely to win. Hence it must be rational to believe that it is very unlikely that any of the thousand tickets will win – that is, rational to believe that it is very unlikely that there will be a winning ticket.

THE PREFACE

Knowing one's frailties as one does, it is rational to suppose that one's book contains errors, and it is not unknown for authors to say as much in their prefaces. However, a sincere author will believe everything asserted in the text. Rationality, plus modesty, thus forces such an author to a contradiction. (Cf. Makinson [1965].)

THE PREFACE AGAIN

Suppose an author's preface consists solely in this remark: "At least one statement in this book is false." Then the body of the book must contain at least one false statement. For suppose it does not: Then if the preface is true, it is false, and if it is false, it is true; which is impossible. (Cf. Prior [1961], pp. 85–6.)

THE INFALLIBLE SEDUCER

An unsuccessful wooer was advised to ask his beloved the following two questions:

1. Will you answer this question in the same way that you will answer the next?
2. Will you sleep with me?

If she keeps her word, she must answer Yes to the second question whatever she has answered to the first.

This paradox is amusingly generalized in Storer [1961].

BURIDAN'S TENTH SOPHISM

Suppose that:

A is thinking that $2 + 2 = 4$.
B is thinking that dogs are reptiles.
C is thinking that an odd number of the current thoughts of A,
     B, and C are true.

Is what C thinks true or not? (See Buridan, in Hughes [1982], p. 85, Prior [1961], Burge [1978], p. 28.)

FORRESTER'S PARADOX

Suppose Smith is going to murder Jones. It is obligatory that if he murders Jones, he should do so gently. This appears to imply that if Smith murders Jones, it is obligatory that he do so gently. However, he cannot murder Jones gently without murdering him. Hence, given that Smith is going to murder Jones, it is obligatory that he do so. (See Forrester [1984].)

THE CHOOSER

Someone whom you trust implicitly presents you with a choice: You can take either or both of box A or box B. Whatever happens, there is $100 in box B; moreover, there will be in addition $10,000 dollars in box A if and only if you choose irrationally. What should you do? (Cf. Gaifman [1983].)

BERTRAND'S PARADOX

What is the probability that a random chord of a circle exceeds the side of an inscribed equilateral triangle? It is longer if its midpoint lies on the inner half of the radius bisecting it; so, since the midpoint may lie anywhere on this radius, the probability is one-half (.5). It is also longer if its midpoint lies within a concentric circle with half the original radius; so, since the area of this inner circle is a quarter that of the original circle, the probability is one-quarter (.25).

*THIS IS NONSENSE

Line 1: The sentence written on Line 1 is nonsense.

Line 2: The sentence written on Line 1 is nonsense.

For a suitable interpretation of "nonsense," we incline to believe that the sentence on Line 2 is true: The sentence it refers to is viciously self-referential, deserves to fall in the truth-value gap, or whatever. Yet the sentence on Line 2 is the very sentence it so justly criticizes.

The example is due to Gaifman [1983].

APPENDIX II
REMARKS ON SOME TEXT
QUESTIONS AND APPENDED
PARADOXES

Remark numbers refer to footnote numbers in the given chapter.

CHAPTER 1

2.   One possible argument is this. If there were as many as two things, say α and β, then we could consider the whole ω formed by these two things. Then ω has α and β as its parts. So if nothing has parts, there are not as many as two things, i.e., there is at most one thing.

9.   Yes, it does mean that the button will travel faster than the speed of light. Whether or not this is a logical possibility could be disputed, but it is fairly uncontroversial that it is not impossible *a priori;* that is, reasoning alone, unaided by experiment, cannot establish that nothing can travel faster than light.

13. "Going out of existence at Z^*" might mean "Z^* was the last point occupied" or, alternatively, "Z^* was the first point not occupied." The latter serves Benacerraf's cause against the objection.

CHAPTER 3

3.   If a person's utilities can be measured in cash value terms, then his or her utilities are "commensurable": Of any two possible circumstances, either one has more utility than the other, or else they are of equal utility. However, if we think of very disparate "utilities," it may be not merely that

151

we do not *know* how they compare, but that there is no such thing as how they compare. For an early defense of commensurability see Rashdall [1907], chap. 2. For a recent discussion see Nussbaum [1986], passim and esp. p. 107ff.

4.   It would seem that it could not as it stands, for the following reason. The outcome of a gamble, in cash terms, does not register the fact that it is obtained by gambling. A given sum has the utility it has, whether earned or won. So what would be needed, to register a dislike of gambling, would be a "higher-order" conception of utility. The expected utilities delivered by the MEU as it stands would be subjected to a weighting, which would augment expected utilities whose probability component is high, and diminish those whose probability component is low.

20.   Each reasons as follows: "In the *last* game it will be best for me to confess, since any loss of trust this induces will be irrelevant, as we are not going to 'play' again." However, the other can work this out and will adopt the same strategy: "Since he will confess in the *last* game, I should confess in the penultimate game, since any loss of trust this may induce will be irrelevant" (and so on).

CHAPTER 4

3.   It might be that the conditions for evidence being good could not be known to obtain.

9.   "All emeralds are green" and "All emeralds are grue" are not, strictly, inconsistent. If there were no unexamined emeralds, both generalizations would be true; whereas it is impossible for genuinely inconsistent propositions both to be true.

A given body of evidence can "point both ways," i.e., can provide grounds for two propositions that are genuinely inconsistent. In such cases, the evidence can normally be divided into evidence that supports the one proposition, and evidence that supports the other, without overlap (at least, without total overlap). What is paradoxical about the grue case is that no such division is possible: Divide the evidence as fine as you like, every bit that confirms "All emeralds are green" also confirms "All emeralds are grue."

CHAPTER 5

11. Suppose L_1 is false; then it tells it the way it is, so it is true, and hence *L_1 is not false*. (Principle: Anything true is not false.) So not-L_1 is true, as the italicized sentence shows, and therefore L_1 is false. (Principle: Anything whose negation is true is false.) Collecting our results: L_1 is not false and L_1 is false. (Cf. Martin [1984], pp. 2–3.)

APPENDIX I

The Grid

The alleged paradox seems to turn on an equivocation between whether there is a sequence of moves that fixes one's position, and whether every possible sequence does so. There is no corresponding equivocation in the Unexpected Examination. (But see Sorenson [1982].)

The Stone

No, an omnipotent being cannot make a stone so heavy that he cannot lift it. He will still be omnipotent with respect to making and lifting stones, however, if for any weight of stone (in grams, megatons, or whatever) he can make one of that weight and lift one of that weight.

The Lottery

One suggestion is that this shows the following: One may have good reason for believing that *A* and good reason for believing that *B*, yet not have good reason for believing that *A* and *B*. This suggestion would need to be supplemented by a treatment of sorites-style reasoning based on: "If one has good reason to believe a proposition with probability *n*, then one has good reason to believe a proposition with probability minutely smaller than *n*."

This Is Nonsense

The example supports the view that two sentence-tokens of a single sentence-type can differ in truth value (one true, the other not) even if both refer to the same thing and predicate the same property of it.

This view, suggested by Gaifman [1983], would enable one to hold that L_2 (see section 5.2) is true even though (a) L_1 is not true, and (b) L_2 refers to the very same thing as L_1 and predicates the very same property of it.

BIBLIOGRAPHY

Aristotle. *Physics* Trans. W. Charlton. Oxford University Press, Oxford. 1970.

Asher, Nicholas M., and Kamp, Johan A. W. [1986] "The knower's paradox and representational theories of the attitudes." In J. Halpern, ed. *Theoretical Aspects of Reasoning about Knowledge*. Morgan Kaufman, New York, pp. 131–48.

Axelrod, R. [1984] *The Evolution of Cooperation*. Basic Books, New York.

Bar-Hillel, Maya, and Margalit, Avishai [1972] "Newcomb's paradox revisited." *British Journal for Philosophy of Science* 23: 295–304.

Barwise, Jon, and Etchemendy, John [1987] *The Liar: An Essay in Truth and Circularity*. Oxford University Press, New York & Oxford.

Benacerraf, Paul [1962] "Tasks, super-tasks, and the modern Eleatics." *Journal of Philosophy* 59: 765–84. Reprinted in W. Salmon [1970], pp. 103–29.

Benditt, T.M., and Ross, David J. [1976] "Newcomb's paradox." *British Journal for the Philosophy of Science* 27: 161–4.

Black, Max [1937] "Vagueness: an exercise in logical analysis." *Philosophy of Science* 4: 427–55. Reprinted in his *Language and Philosophy*. Cornell University Press, Ithaca, N.Y. 1949.

[1967] "Probability." In Edwards [1967], pp. 464–79.

Burge, Tyler [1978] "Buridan and epistemic paradox." *Philosophical Studies* 34: 21–35.

[1979] "Semantical paradox." *The Journal of Philosophy* 76: 169–98. Reprinted in Martin [1984], pp. 83–117.

[1984] "Epistemic paradox." *The Journal of Philosophy* 81: 5–29.

Buridan, John *Sophismata*, trans. and ed. Hughes [1982].

Campbell, Richmond, and Sowden, Lanning, eds. [1985] *Paradoxes of Rationality and Cooperation: Prisoner's Dilemma and Newcomb's Problem*. University of British Columbia Press, Vancouver.

Dummett, Michael [1975] "Wang's paradox." *Synthese* 30: 301–24. Reprinted in his *Truth and Other Enigmas*. Duckworth, London. 1978, pp. 248–68.

155

Edwards, Paul [1967] *The Encyclopedia of Philosophy*. Collier–Macmillan and The Free Press, New York.

Evans, Gareth [1978] "Can there be vague objects?" *Analysis* 38: 208. Reprinted in his *Collected Papers*. Oxford University Press, Oxford. 1985, pp. 176–7.

Fine, Kit [1975] "Vagueness, truth and logic." *Synthese* 30: 265–300.

Forrester, James William [1984] "Gentle murder and the adverbial samaritan." *Journal of Philosophy* 81: 193–97.

Foster, John [1983] "Induction, explanation and natural necessity." *Proceedings of the Aristotelian Society* 83: 87–101.

Foster, Marguerite, and Martin, Michael L., eds. [1966] *Probability, Confirmation and Simplicity*. Odyssey Press, New York.

Gaifman, Haim [1983] "Paradoxes of infinity and self-application, I." *Erkenntnis* 20: 131–55.

Gale, Richard M., ed. [1968] *The Philosophy of Time*. Macmillan, London.

Gibbard, A., and Harper, W.L. [1978] "Counterfactuals and two kinds of expected utility." In C. A. Hooker, J. J. Leach, and E. F. McClennon, eds. *Foundations and Applications of Decision Theory*, vol. I. Reidel, Dordrecht, pp. 125–62. Reprinted (abridged) in Campbell and Sowden [1985], pp. 133–58.

Goguen, J.A. [1969] "The logic of inexact concepts." *Synthese* 19: 325–78.

Goodman, Nelson [1955] *Fact, Fiction and Forecast*. Harvard University Press, Cambridge, Mass.; 2nd ed., Bobbs-Merrill, Indianapolis, 1965.

[1978] *Ways of Worldmaking*. Hackett, Indianapolis.

Grünbaum, Adolf [1967] *Modern Science and Zeno's Paradoxes*. Wesleyan University Press, Middletown, Conn.

Gupta, Anil [1982] "Truth and paradox." *Journal of Philosophical Logic* 11: 1–60. Reprinted in Martin [1984], pp. 175–235.

Hempel, Carl [1945] *Aspects of Scientific Explanation and Other Essays in the Philosophy of Science*. The Free Press, New York. Reprint ed., 1965. (The material on the Ravens Paradox is reprinted from *Mind* 54: 1–26, 97–121 [1945]).

Hertzberger, Hans A. [1970] "Paradoxes of grounding in semantics." *The Journal of Philosophy* 67: 145–67.

Hughes, G. E., ed. and trans. [1982] *John Buridan on Self-Reference*. Cambridge University Press, Cambridge & New York. This work by Buridan was originally entitled *Sophismata*.

Hume, David [1738] *A Treatise of Human Nature*.

Jackson, Frank [1975] "Grue." *Journal of Philosophy* 72: 113–31.

Jeffrey, Richard C. [1965] *The Logic of Decision*. McGraw-Hill, New York.

Kamp, Hans [1981] "The paradox of the heap." In U. Monnich, ed. *Aspects of Philosophical Logic*. Reidel, Dordrecht, pp. 225–77.

Kripke, Saul [1975] "Outline of a theory of truth." *The Journal of Philosophy* 72: 690–716. Reprinted in Martin [1984], 53–81.

[1982] *Wittgenstein on Rules and Private Language*. Blackwell, Oxford.

Kyburg, Henry [1961] *Probability and the Logic of Rational Belief*. Wesleyan University Press, Middletown, Conn.

Levi, Isaac [1967] *Gambling with Truth*. RKP, London.

Lewis, David [1979] "Prisoner's Dilemma is a Newcomb Problem." *Philosophy and Public Affairs* 8: 235–40. Reprinted in Campbell and Sowden [1985], pp. 251–5.

Mackie, J. L.. [1977] "Newcomb's paradox and the direction of causation." *Canadian Philosophical Review* 7: 213–25. Reprinted in his *Collected Papers II*.

Makinson, D. C. [1965] "The paradox of the preface." *Analysis* 25: 205–7.

Martin, Robert L., ed. [1984] *Recent Essays on Truth and the Liar Paradox*. Oxford University Press, Oxford.

Mellor, D.H. [1971] *The Matter of Chance*. Cambridge University Press, Cambridge & New York.

Montague, Richard, and Kaplan, David [1960] "A paradox regained." *Notre Dame Journal of Formal Logic* 1: 79–90. Reprinted in Richmond Thomason, ed., *Formal Philosophy*. Yale University Press, New Haven. 1974, pp. 271–85.

Nozick, R. [1969] "Newcomb's problem and two principles of choice." In Nicholas Rescher, ed. *Essays in Honor of Carl G. Hempel*. Reidel, Dordrecht. Abridged version reprinted in Campbell and Sowden [1985], pp. 107–33.

Nussbaum, Martha C. [1986] *The Fragility of Goodness: Luck and Ethics in Greek Tragedy and Philosophy*. Cambridge University Press, Cambridge & New York.

Parfit, Derek [1984] *Reasons and Persons*. Oxford University Press, Oxford.

Peacocke, C. A. B. [1981] "Are vague predicates incoherent?" *Synthese* 46: 121–41.

Peirce, C. [1935] *The Collected Papers of Charles Sanders Peirce*. Charles Hartshorne and Paul Weiss, eds. Harvard University Press, Cambridge, Mass.

Priest, Graham [1986] "Contradiction, belief and rationality." *Proceedings of the Aristotelian Society* 86: 99–116.

Priest, Graham, Routley, R., and Norman, J., eds. [1985] *Paraconsistent Logic*. Philosophia Verlag, Munich.

Prior, Arthur N. [1961] "On a family of paradoxes." *Notre Dame Journal of Formal Logic* 2: 16–32.

[1971] *Objects of Thought.* Oxford University Press, Oxford.

Quine, Willard van O. [1953] "On a so-called paradox." *Mind* 62: 65–7. Reprinted in his [1966], pp. 19–21.

[1966] *Ways of Paradox and Other Essays.* Random House, New York. (The title essay is on pp. 1–18.)

Ramsey, Frank P. [1925] "The foundations of mathematics." Reprinted in D. H. Mellor, ed. *Foundations.* Humanities Press, Atlantic Highlands, N.J. 1978, pp. 152–212.

[1926] "Truth and probability." Reprinted in D.H. Mellor, ed. *Foundations.* Humanities Press, Atlantic Highlands, N.J. 1978, pp. 58–100.

Rashdall, Hastings [1907] *The Theory of Good and Evil,* vol. II. Oxford University Press, London.

Rescher, N., and Brandom, R. [1980] *The Logic of Inconsistency.* Blackwell, Oxford.

Russell, Bertrand [1903] *The Principles of Mathematics.* Cambridge University Press, Cambridge & New York.

[1908] "Mathematical logic as based on the theory of types." *American Journal of Mathematics* 30: 222–62. Reprinted in R. C. Marsh, ed. *Logic and Knowledge.* Allen and Unwin, London. 1956, pp. 59–102.

[1910] Introduction to *Principia Mathematica.* Cambridge University Press, Cambridge & New York. (Joint authorship with A. N. Whitehead for the *Principia* itself.)

[1936] "The Limits of Empiricism." *Proceedings of the Aristotelian Society* 36: 131–50.

Salmon, Nathan U. [1982] *Reference and Essence.* Blackwell, Oxford.

Salmon, Wesley C. [1970] *Zeno's Paradoxes.* Bobbs-Merrill, Indianapolis.

[1980] *Space, Time and Motion: A Philosophical Introduction.* University of Minnesota Press, Minneapolis. 2nd ed.

Sanford, D. [1976] "Competing semantics of vagueness: many values vs. super-truth." *Synthese* 33: 195–210.

Savage, C. Wade [1967] "The paradox of the stone." *Philosophical Review* 76: 74–9.

Schlesinger, G. [1974a] *Confirmation and Confirmability.* Oxford University Press, New York.

[1974b] "The unpredictability of free choice." *British Journal for the Philosophy of Science* 25: 209–21.

Schrader, David E. [1979] "A solution to the stone paradox." *Synthese* 42: 255–64.

Selton, Reinhard [1978] "The chain store paradox." *Theory and Decision* 9: 127–59.

Skyrms, Brian [1982] "Intensional aspects of semantical self-reference." In Martin [1984], pp. 119–31.

Sorenson, Roy A. [1982] "Recalcitrant variations of the prediction paradox." *Australasian Journal of Philosophy* 60: 355–62.

Stack, Michael F. [1977] "A solution to the predictor paradox." *Canadian Journal of Philosophy* 7: 147–54.

Storer, Thomas [1961] "MINIAC: World's smallest electronic brain." *Analysis* 22: 151–2.

Tarski, Alfred [1937] "The concept of truth in formalized languages." In his *Logic, Semantics, Metamathematics*. Clarendon Press, New York. 1956, pp. 152–278.

[1969] "Truth and Proof." *Scientific American* 194: 63–77.

Thomson, James F. [1954] "Tasks and super-tasks." *Analysis* 15: 1–13. Reprinted in Richard M. Gale [1968], pp. 406–21, and in W. C. Salmon [1970], 89–102.

Unger, Peter [1979] "I do not exist." In Graham MacDonald, ed. *Perception and Identity: Essays Presented to A.J. Ayer*. Macmillan, London. 1979.

van Fraassen, B. [1966] "Singular terms, truth-value gaps, and free logic." *Journal of Philosophy* 53: 481–85.

[1968] "Presupposition, implication and self-reference." *Journal of Philosophy* 65: 136–52.

van Heijenoort, John [1967] "Logical paradoxes." In Edwards [1967], vol. 5, pp. 44–51.

Vlastos, Gregory [1967] "Zeno of Elea." In Edwards [1967], vol. 8, pp. 369–79.

Wiggins, David [1986] "On singling out an object determinately." In Philip Pettit and John McDowell, eds. *Subject, Thought, and Context*. Oxford University Press, Oxford, pp. 169–80.

Wright, Crispin [1975] "On the coherence of vague predicates." *Synthese* 30: 325–65.

[1976] "Language-mastery and the sorites paradox." In Gareth Evans and John McDowell, eds. *Truth and Meaning*. Oxford University Press, Oxford, pp. 223–47.

Wright, Crispin, and Sudbury, Aidan [1977] "The paradox of the unexpected examination." *Australasian Journal of Philosophy* 60: 41–58.

INDEX

161